SUPERANNUATION & **TAXATION**

A Practical Guide to Saving Tax on Your Super or SMSF

Jimmy B. Prince

Wrightbooks

First published 2011 by Wrightbooks
an imprint of John Wiley & Sons Australia, Ltd
42 McDougall Street, Milton Qld 4064

Office also in Melbourne

Typeset in Adobe Garamond 12.5/15.5pt

© Jimmy B. Prince 2011

The moral rights of the author have been asserted

National Library of Australia Cataloguing-in-Publication entry

Author:	Prince, Jimmy B.
Title:	Superannuation and taxation: a practical guide to saving tax on your super or SMSF / Jimmy B. Prince.
ISBN:	9780730376750 (pbk.)
Notes:	Includes index.
Subjects:	Pensions — Taxation — Australia.
	Pension trusts — Taxation — Australia.
	Saving and investment — Australia.
Dewey Number:	331.2520994

Cover image ($100 note) © iStockphoto.com/robynmac

Tables 8.1 and 8.2 © Australian Taxation Office. The ATO material included in this publication was current at the time of publishing. Readers should refer to the ATO website <www.ato.gov.au> for up-to-date ATO information. All extracts taken from Australian Acts of Law © Commonwealth of Australia 2011. All legislation herein is reproduced by permission but does not purport to be the official or authorised version. It is subject to Commonwealth of Australia copyright. The *Copyright Act 1968* permits certain reproduction and publication of Commonwealth legislation and judgements. In particular, section 182A of the Act enables a complete copy to be made by or on behalf of a particular person. For reproduction or publication beyond that permitted by the Act, permission should be sought in writing. Requests should be addressed to Commonwealth Copyright Administration, Attorney-General's Department, Robert Garran Offices, National Circuit, Bardon, ACT 2600, or posted at http://www.ag.gov.au/cca.

Printed in Australia by Ligare Book Printer

10 9 8 7 6 5 4 3 2 1

Disclaimer

The material in this publication is of the nature of general comment only, and does not represent professional advice. It is not intended to provide specific guidance for particular circumstances and it should not be relied on as the basis for any decision to take action or not take action on any matter which it covers. Readers should obtain professional advice where appropriate, before making any such decision. To the maximum extent permitted by law, the author and publisher disclaim all responsibility and liability to any person, arising directly or indirectly from any person taking or not taking action based upon the information in this publication.

Contents

About the author

Jim Prince is a fellow of CPA Australia and a tax specialist. He is a former lecturer and tutor in income tax law at LaTrobe University and teaches a number of wealth-creation courses for the Centre for Adult Education in Melbourne. He has authored several investment books, including *Tax for Australians for Dummies, Shares & Taxation* and *Property & Taxation,* and has written articles for *Your Mortgage* magazine and <http://thebull.com. au>. In 2000 Jim was nominated for an Adult Learners Week 2000 outstanding tutor award.

In his earlier years Jim worked for the Australian Taxation Office and also consulted to CPA Australia 'TechniCALL'.

Preface

When compulsory superannuation was introduced in Australia in the 1990s, the federal government was sending a clear message to everyone that they had to fund their own retirement. To encourage you to participate in super, the government has introduced a number of tax concessions that may interest you. One such benefit comes when you reach 60 years of age and retire: you pay no tax then on all pensions and lump sum withdrawals, and they are both excluded from your assessable income. The amount you accumulate in your superannuation fund will ultimately determine the quality of your lifestyle in your old age. So it's prudent that you make a contribution each financial year while you're still gainfully employed.

Relying on the old age pension to subsidise your lifestyle in retirement is no longer a viable option, unless you can convince Centrelink that you're destitute. To qualify for the old age pension you need to satisfy a strict income test and asset test. These tests check whether the total income you derive each financial year and the amount of assets you currently own fall within acceptable statutory limits. To make reliance on the age pension more difficult, the federal government plans to progressively increase the age for eligibility for the old age pension to 67 years by 2023.

The *Income Tax Assessment Act 1997* permits individuals to set up and manage their own superannuation fund. Although you can gain significant tax benefits from managing your own super fund, like all good things in life it comes at a cost. There are strict rules and regulations you need to comply with, and there are stiff financial and criminal penalties in place if you contravene them. You also need to determine at the outset whether you can outperform the professionally managed funds to make your own super fund a viable and worthwhile exercise. So it's important that you understand your duties and responsibilities and know that you're capable of investing your money wisely.

The purpose of writing this book is to explain how the Australian superannuation system works, and more particularly the various statutory provisions you need to comply with if you want to set up and run a self managed superannuation fund (SMSF). The book explains in simple terms the core tax principles relating to superannuation funds, and offers numerous tax tips, points out potential tax traps and includes practical case studies to help you to save paying tax. You'll also find a comprehensive list of legal citations to all the major tax cases relating to superannuation transactions. Much emphasis is placed on the following points:

- how the Australian superannuation system works and the benefits you can gain

- how much you need to accumulate to fund your own retirement

- how to set up an SMSF

- the rules and regulations you need to comply with if you want to manage your own super fund

- the rules associated with making a superannuation contribution

- how superannuation funds are taxed

- how to invest your money wisely

- the rules you need to satisfy to access your preserved benefits

- how superannuation pensions and death benefits are taxed.

Throughout the book you'll have at your fingertips instant, at a glance, information about core tax principles, plus references to tax publications, tax rulings and tax determinations that tax professionals use to solve specific problems. You can quickly find these Tax Office publications and rulings on the Australian Taxation Office website <www.ato.gov.au>. You can refer to this practical guide at any time to find a particular publication or ruling to help you save tax on your super or SMSF.

Chapter 1

The superannuation scheme: removing the mystique

Superannuation is an investment vehicle that you can use to help you save for your retirement. The federal government has introduced a number of tax incentives to encourage you to do so. The sole purpose of having a superannuation fund must be to provide benefits to members upon retirement, and benefits to dependants in the event of a member's death. The amount you accumulate in your super fund will ultimately determine the standard of living you can expect to have in your old age. So it's best that you understand how the system works. In this chapter, I provide an overview of the Australian superannuation scheme and the various tax benefits you can gain.

How you're taxed in Australia

Under Australian tax law, tax is levied on your taxable income—'total assessable income less allowable deductions equals taxable income'. At the end of the financial year—which commences on 1 July and ends on 30 June—an Australian resident is statutorily obliged to lodge a tax return disclosing the taxable income they derive from all sources, whether within or outside of Australia. If you're running a self managed superannuation fund (SMSF), you need to lodge a *Self managed superannuation fund annual return* disclosing the taxable income your super fund derived during the financial year (see chapter 6).

Coming to terms with self-assessment

The Australian tax system operates on a self-assessment basis (or honour system). This means that, when you lodge your annual tax return, the Australian Taxation Office or ATO (the federal government authority responsible for administering Australia's tax laws) will ordinarily accept its contents as being true and correct. Apart from correcting any noticeable errors (for instance, mistakes in adding up) no further action is taken. However, to keep you honest, the Tax Office conducts routine tax audits and data-matching checks, through which information disclosed in your tax return is matched with information from various external sources (such as records supplied by the banks of interest earned). This is to check whether you're complying with the Income Tax Assessment

Act. Stiff penalties may apply if you're found to have understated your assessable income or overstated your allowable deductions. The onus is on you to comply.

If you plan to run an SMSF, each year you must appoint an independent auditor (at your own expense!) before you can lodge your super fund's annual tax return. This is to check that you're not cooking the books and that you're complying with the *Superannuation Industry (Supervision) Act 1993* (SIS Act). The auditor must report any significant contraventions to the Tax Office. So it's important that you understand your legal obligations and responsibilities (see chapter 4).

Under self-assessment, if you're not sure about a particular tax issue you can seek a private ruling from the Tax Office. This is a free service to taxpayers, where the Tax Office will give you a written response as to how they would interpret the tax law in respect of the tax matter you raised. For more details see the Tax Office publication *How to apply for a private ruling*.

 Tax tip

The Tax Office regularly issues income tax rulings, tax determinations, ATO interpretative decisions and educational fact sheets to explain various tax matters (particularly superannuation). These publications are all free of charge and you can find them on the ATO website <www.ato.gov.au>. See also the 'Useful references' at the end of each chapter.

Tax tip

The trustee of an SMSF must lodge a *Self managed superannuation fund annual return* by 31 October. You may be charged a late lodgement penalty if you fail to comply. You can avoid this penalty if a registered tax agent prepares your return. This is because tax agents are given a general extension of time to lodge tax returns on behalf of their clients.

Four types of super funds

The sole purpose of having a superannuation fund must be to provide benefits to members upon retirement (or permanent disability), and benefits to dependants in the event of a member's death. There are four different types of super funds that you can make super contributions to in order to achieve this objective. They are referred to as:

- *Public sector funds.* These are super funds that have been set up specifically for public servants who work for the federal or state and territory governments of Australia. You may be ineligible to become a member of some of these funds unless you're a government employee. AGEST Super, for instance, is a major super fund for members who work for the Commonwealth government.

- *Retail super funds.* These are super funds that have been specifically set up by Australia's leading financial institutions, such as banks and life insurance companies. Anyone can become a member of a retail super fund. Retail funds ordinarily provide a wide choice of investment options (in various asset classes) to their members to help maximise benefits. In return, they will charge you management and administration fees for looking after your money. If you want more information about retail super funds, visit the Association of Superannuation Funds of Australia (ASFA) website <www.superannuation.asn.au>.

- *Industry super funds.* These super funds were originally set up for employees of specific industries. They are not-for-profit super funds and now anyone can become a member of most industry funds. The management and administration fees they charge to look after your benefits are ordinarily lower than those charged by retail funds, and their policy is not to pay commissions to financial advisers. For more information you can visit the Industry Super Funds website <www.industrysuper.com>. The major industry super funds you can choose from include:

  □ Accountants Super (accounting profession)

  □ Cbus (construction industry)

  □ Hesta Super Fund (health and community services sector)

  □ Host Plus (hospitality, tourism, recreation and sport sector)

  □ MTAA Super Fund (motor trade industry)

- ◻ Media Super (print, media, entertainment and arts sector)

- ◻ NGS Super (non-government education sector)

- ◻ Legal Super (legal sector)

- ◻ REI Super (property sector).

- *Self managed superannuation funds (SMSFs).* These are super funds that are set up by individuals who would prefer to manage their own super fund. It's generally considered you need to have about $250 000 in super to make this a viable option. You need to comply with stringent rules if you want to set up and run your own super fund. And if you don't agree to be regulated or you fail to meet these stringent rules, there's a risk your fund could become a non-complying super fund. If this happened, you will not qualify for certain tax concessions, and your fund is liable to pay tax at the rate of 45 per cent (rather than 15 per cent if your fund is a complying super fund). (For more details, see chapters 3 and 4.)

 Tax tip

You can also make a superannuation contribution to a retirement savings account (RSA). RSAs are government-guaranteed savings accounts that are offered by Australia's leading financial institutions, such as banks, credit unions and life assurance companies. An RSA earns interest, and the management and administration fees to manage your money are minimal. An RSA account can be used to pay you a pension on retirement. You need to supply your tax file number (TFN) when you open an RSA.

Reading the fine print: what you need to do

As there are numerous super funds eager to get hold of your money, it's best that you check out the super fund's product disclosure statement (PDS) before you choose a particular fund. This is a legal document that will set out relevant information, such as:

- the different types of fees and charges the fund will charge to manage your accumulated benefits, the amount you're likely to pay each year, and how fees and charges are calculated

- the different types of investment options you can select, and, more particularly, the investment and asset allocation policy followed to maximise member benefits (see The accumulation phase on p. 15); the investment choices available are a major factor when weighing up whether you should choose a retail fund or industry fund, or whether you should manage your own SMSF

- the death and disability insurance cover you can tap into

- the various services super funds offer their members (for instance, online access to member account details and free education material).

The Australian Securities & Investments Commission (ASIC) consumer website <www.moneysmart.gov.au> has a handy publication *Super funds comparison worksheet* to help you compare the different types of super funds. The ultimate test as to whether you should choose a retail fund or industry fund is the funds capacity to consistently generate a good yield on your investment, in return for the fees you must pay it to manage your money. It goes without saying that, the better it performs, the more money you will have when you retire. Incidentally, if you're dissatisfied with your fund's performance or feel the fees are too high, you can roll over (transfer) your benefits to another complying super fund (see chapter 5). Alternatively, if you decide to set up an SMSF, you need to determine whether you can outperform the various professionally managed funds from which you can choose.

Taking that first step: making a contribution

To get the ball rolling you need to make a contribution to a superannuation fund or an RSA. In the mid 1990s the federal government introduced a compulsory superannuation scheme to help employees fund their own retirement.

Under the superannuation guarantee legislation, if you're an employee, your employer has a statutory obligation to contribute 9 per cent of your ordinary time earnings (gross pay) into a complying super fund of your choice. An employee can include a director of a company. For example, if you earn $1000 a week, your employer must contribute $90 to your nominated super fund ($1000 × 9 per cent = $90). If you don't choose a super fund, your employer will ordinarily choose a default fund for you (see MySuper on p. 18). To help build your nest egg the federal government intends to progressively increase the superannuation guarantee rate from 9 per cent to 12 per cent by 2019–20; see appendix A, table 11. As your employer can claim a tax deduction for making a concessional contribution (or before-tax contribution) on your behalf, your super fund treats the superannuation guarantee contributions as assessable contributions, and it pays a 15 per cent contributions tax (see chapter 6), which is deducted from your super account.

 Tax tip

When you commence employment you need to complete a *Choice of superannuation fund standard choice form* (NAT 13080). You also need to certify that your choice of super fund is a complying super fund in accordance with superannuation laws in order to qualify for tax concessions. All the professionally managed super funds that operate in Australia are

Tax tip *(cont'd)*

complying super funds. This only becomes an issue if you plan to set up an SMSF (see chapter 3). If you don't make a choice, your employer will choose a default super fund for you. For more information see the Tax Office publication *Choosing a super fund—How to complete your standard choice form.*

 Tax tip

When you join a complying super fund you need to supply your TFN. Although this is not compulsory, if you don't supply the number, you could be liable to pay additional income tax on your employer super guarantee contributions, salary sacrifice contributions and personal pre-tax concessional contributions. And you may be ineligible to made non-concessional (or after-tax) contributions to your super fund. For more details see the Tax Office publication *No tax file number (TFN) contributions.*

Individuals who are self-employed or substantially self-employed are given tax incentives to encourage them to make personal superannuation contributions. The carrot here is that the concessional (pre-tax) contributions they make to a complying super fund qualify for a tax deduction.

Incidentally, under Australian tax law a deduction is allowed in the financial year the contribution is made. As these contributions are tax deductible; your super fund treats the contribution as an assessable contribution, and will pay a 15 per cent contributions tax, which is deducted from your account (as is the case with employer super guarantee contributions). (See chapter 6 for more information.)

The federal government has also introduced a number of tax incentives to help boost the accumulated benefits of low-income earners (see chapter 5). You can also make non-concessional, or after-tax, contributions (see chapter 5). As these contributions do not qualify for a tax deduction, your super fund does not pay a 15 per cent contributions tax, as is the case if you make a concessional contribution.

At a glance: the tax benefits you can gain

The major tax benefits you can gain from contributing to a complying super fund (and more particularly an SMSF) are listed here.

Taxation

- Super funds are liable to pay a 15 per cent rate of tax on investment earnings and concessional contributions that qualify for a tax deduction. But the amount of tax payable is reduced if your super fund receives dividend franking credits (see chapter 6).

- Your super fund (and more particularly an SMSF) can offer you death and disability insurance cover and the cost is a tax-deductible expense (see chapter 6).

Contributions

- A self-employed or substantially self-employed person can make personal pre-tax concessional contributions to a complying super fund. The payment (up to a cap amount) is a tax-deductible expense (see chapter 6).

- An employee can salary sacrifice some of their pre-tax salary (up to a cap amount) into a complying super fund and save paying income tax on the amount contributed (see chapter 5).

- You can make personal after-tax non-concessional contributions (up to a cap amount) if you're less than 65 years of age. But you need to satisfy an employment test (work a specific number of hours over a set period of days) if you're over 65 years of age (see chapter 5).

- A government superannuation co-contribution scheme aims to encourage low-income earners to make a contribution to a complying super fund. Under this scheme the government will make a co-contribution into your super fund if you make an after-tax non-concessional contribution up to a cap amount (see chapter 5).

- Tax incentives aim to encourage you to make a personal after-tax non-concessional contribution on behalf of your spouse. This is called a spouse contribution (see chapter 5).

- You can split concessional contributions you make to a complying super fund with your spouse (see chapter 6).

- If you operate a small business you can gain capital gains tax relief if you transfer capital gains you make on sale of active (business) assets to your complying super fund (see chapter 6).

Pensions

- When you reach your preservation age (currently 55 years of age), you can elect to receive a transition to retirement pension from your super while you're still gainfully employed (see chapter 8).

- Pensions payable to members who are between 55 and 59 years of age ordinarily qualify for a 15 per cent tax offset. For instance, if you receive a $40 000 pension you can claim a $6000 tax offset (see chapter 8).

- Pensions and lump sum payments payable to members after they turn 60 years of age are ordinarily free of tax, and are excluded from their assessable income (see chapter 8).

- Investment earnings and capital gains on the sale of investment assets to fund pension options during the pension phase in a super fund are free of tax (see chapter 8).

At a glance: limitations of putting money into super

The major limitations of putting money into a super fund are listed here.

- Super funds are liable to pay a 15 per cent rate of tax on concessional contributions they receive from members (see chapter 5).

- Members cannot access their preserved benefits until they satisfy a condition of release; for instance, when they reach their preservation age and retire (see chapter 8).

- Members are liable to pay account-keeping fees on their super account.

- Stiff penalties apply if you operate an SMSF and contravene the SIS Act (see chapter 4).

- Statutory limits restrict the amount of concessional and non-concessional contributions you can make to a complying super fund each year. Excess contributions are liable to a 46.5 per cent rate of tax (see chapter 5).

 Tax tip

Under the *Same-Sex Relationships (Equal Treatment in Commonwealth Laws—Superannuation)* Act 2008, same-sex couples are eligible to receive the same tax benefits and superannuation concessions that are available to married and opposite-sex de facto couples. Furthermore, children of same-sex couples are treated in the same way as children in a marriage. For more details see the Tax Office publication *Same-Sex Relationships (Equal Treatment in Common-wealth Laws—Superannuation)*.

The two phases of superannuation

There are two distinct phases in the life cycle of a complying super fund. They are commonly referred to as:

- the accumulation phase
- the pension phase.

Each phase has certain tax rules and regulations that the fund needs to comply with. And there are stiff penalties if these are contravened by the fund, or you, if you have an SMSF. Incidentally, the term complying super fund means a fund that has agreed to be regulated under the SIS Act. Only complying super funds can qualify for tax concessions.

The accumulation phase

The money that is contributed to your super fund each year is invested on your behalf. The investment earnings your fund derives are liable to a 15 per cent rate of tax, as against paying your marginal tax rate plus a Medicare levy (which can vary between 0 per cent and 46.5 per cent), if you invested the money outside the superannuation system. Your super fund will offer you a number of investment options (or range of asset classes) to help fund your retirement. This information is set out in the super fund's product disclosure statement (PDS), which you need to read at the time you fill in the form to join the fund. The most common investment choices you can select from are listed here:

- *Cash.* This includes investments such as bank bills, fixed interest securities and government bonds. These investments normally pay interest only. They rarely make a loss, but the downside is that your investments are unlikely to appreciate in value.

- *Balanced.* This usually comprises a mixture of investments in shares, fixed interest securities and property. It's called balanced because you are effectively spreading your risk (diversifying) over a number of asset classes, and you will derive regular income, as well as the potential for capital growth.

- *Growth.* In this case your money is predominantly invested in Australian and international share markets, as well as commercial and residential property. These assets normally pay you regular income, as well as the potential for capital growth, but there's a risk they can fall in value.

- *Equity growth.* Your money is invested mainly in shares listed on the Australian Securities Exchange (ASX). These investments normally pay a regular income, and have the potential for capital growth. As these investments are market linked; there's a risk they can fall in value. One significant benefit is that you could receive the benefit of dividend franking credits that can be deducted from the gross tax payable on the taxable income your super fund derives (see chapter 6).

- *Property.* Your money is invested predominantly in commercial and residential property. These investments normally pay you regular income, as well as providing the potential for capital growth.

- *Foreign.* Your money is usually invested in international markets (for instance, the United States, European countries and Asian countries). These investments normally pay you regular income, as well as providing the potential for capital growth.

- *Indexed.* Your money is usually invested in a particular index (for instance, the S&P 200 index, which consists of the top 200 companies and property trusts listed on the ASX). These investments normally pay you regular income and give you the benefit of dividend franking credits, as well as providing the potential for capital growth.

Before you choose a particular investment option, you need to understand how the various investments are likely to perform over a long period of time, and what risks are involved in particular asset classes, as well as the need to diversify (see chapter 7). You will usually find the various investment categories you're offered are market linked, which means they will rise and fall in value in line with the prevailing market. So if you're not sure what investment option to choose, you should seek professional advice. Fund members are normally permitted to switch their investment option at least once a year free of charge. But if you do switch frequently, your super fund may charge you switching fees.

MySuper

If you're a novice or uninterested member or you would rather have someone make all the investment decisions for you, you will soon be able to benefit from a government-approved default superannuation product called MySuper. Incidentally, your employer will be obligated to choose this default option if you do not choose a fund to accept your employer's superannuation guarantee contributions. This is a simplified, low-cost, no-frills super fund investment strategy that must meet certain conditions (and no financial planner commissions or fees are payable). Under this plan your super is invested in a limited choice of investment options with minimum reporting and disclosure. And you will receive basic life and disability cover. It's proposed that MySuper will be offered to super fund members from 1 July 2013.

 Tax tip

All the major super funds regularly issue newsletters to their members, and provide education fact sheets on their respective websites, to explain how the superannuation system works and the various tax benefits you can gain.

Member benefit statements

Complying superannuation funds are legally obliged to issue a member benefit statement each year to their members. The statement will normally provide the following information:

- *Your personal details:* including your name and address, fund member number, the date you joined the fund, your date of birth and whether you have supplied your TFN to the fund.

- *Your investment option choice:* your nominated investment option (for instance, cash, balanced, growth).

- *Your investment's performance:* the rate of return on the investment option you selected, and how it compares with the other investment options you could have chosen.

- *Your insurance benefits:* if you have chosen insurance cover in your fund, the current accumulated death and permanent disability benefit payout balance.

- *Your opening and closing balances:* your opening balance as at a particular date (for instance, 1 July), and your closing balance as at a particular date (for instance, 30 June); you will be anticipating the closing balance will be higher than the opening balance, and if it is not, you need to find out why this is so.

- *Amounts added to your account:* all payments credited to your super fund account from various sources, such as:

  □ contributions, including employer superannuation guarantee contributions; salary sacrifice contributions; self-employed contributions; personal contributions (or non-concessional contributions); superannuation co-contributions; spouse contributions (see chapter 5)

  □ rollovers from other complying superannuation funds (see chapter 5)

  □ investment earnings (see chapter 7).

- *Amounts deducted from your account:* amounts deducted from your account balance, such as income tax; management and administration fees; and death and disability insurance premiums.

- *Your transaction summary:* a summary of the superannuation contributions your super fund received from various sources, and the date they were paid.

- *Description of your benefits:* covers three categories of super benefits, each of which members can legally access under different conditions:

  □ *preserved benefit*—benefits that you can't access until you reach your preservation age and retire; since 1 July 1999 all contributions to super and investment earnings have been classified as preserved benefits.

> ▫ *restricted non-preserved*—benefits that you can access when you retire or satisfy a condition of release (for instance, you terminate your current employment at age 60).

> ▫ *unrestricted non-preserved*—benefits that you can access immediately.

- *Your beneficiary details:* your nominated beneficiary is the person you prefer to receive your benefits in the event of your death, and their details include their relationship to you, and the percentage they stand to receive; this section will also specify whether you have made a binding or non-binding nomination.

Tax tip

If you want your death benefit to be paid to a specific dependant (or to your estate) you need to prepare a binding death benefit nomination form. You can get this form from your super fund. If you do this the trustee *must* follow your instructions and has no discretion to vary your decision. You need to renew this form every three years for your request to remain valid. The trustee of your super fund can assist you with this matter. (Otherwise the fund trustee has the final say on who will get your death benefit.) If you run an SMSF, make sure your instructions are clear and precise, and that they comply with the fund's trust deed; see appendix B, Self managed superannuation funds (death benefit payments).

The pension phase

Although you can gain significant benefits putting money into a complying super fund; the trade-off is you can't access your preserved benefits until you satisfy a condition of release, such as reaching your preservation age and retiring. For instance, if you were born before 1960, your preservation age is 55 years of age, and if you were born after 1964 your preservation age is 60 years of age. You need to adjust if you happen to be born between 1960 and 1964; see appendix A, table 13. When that historic moment in your life occurs, and you decide to retire from the workforce, all investment earnings to fund pension options during the pension phase are exempt from tax, and you have the option to receive a superannuation pension, a superannuation lump sum payment or a combination of the two. To add icing to the retirement cake, once you turn 60, all withdrawals from a complying super fund are exempt from tax and are excluded from your assessable income. Unfortunately, this may not be the case if you're a government employee, but you will qualify for a 10 per cent tax offset (see chapter 8).

Superannuation Complaints Tribunal

If you're dissatisfied with decisions by and the conduct of the trustee of your superannuation fund, you have a right to lodge a written complaint to the Superannuation Complaints Tribunal (SCT). This is a free, independent dispute resolution service to help members resolve certain superannuation-related complaints that were initially raised with the super fund, such as:

- errors appearing in member benefit statements (see Member benefit statements on p. 19)

- unreasonable delays in the payment of benefits to members

- payments of death benefits to beneficiaries (see chapter 9)

- miscalculation of benefit payments or lump sum payments to members

- refusal to approve member claims for a disability payment.

The tribunal cannot consider complaints about a super fund's investment performance, the management of a fund as a whole and employer superannuation contributions. Further, members of an SMSF are ineligible to use this tribunal to resolve disputes arising among the trustees of an SMSF. For more details, visit the Superannuation Complaints Tribunal website <www.sct.gov.au>.

Getting professional help

Federal government websites provide a wealth of information about super. These will help you come to terms with any superannuation issues you're having trouble with. The main ones are listed here.

- *Australian Taxation Office (ATO) <www.ato.gov.au>.*
  The Tax Office is responsible for regulating
  SMSFs. It has prepared a number of user-friendly
  publications to help you understand how the
  superannuation system works, particularly the tax
  rules you need to comply with. These publications
  are free of charge and you can download them from
  the ATO website (see Useful references: Australian
  Taxation Office publications at the end of each
  chapter of this book).

- *Australian Securities & Investments Commission
  (ASIC) consumer website <www.moneysmart.gov.au>.*
  ASIC provides general information about the
  superannuation system, plus financial tips about
  managing your money and getting investment advice.

- *Australian Prudential Regulation Authority (APRA)
  website <www.apra.gov.au>.* APRA is responsible
  for regulating how superannuation funds operate
  (except SMSFs, which are regulated by the Tax
  Office). APRA regularly issues superannuation
  circulars and superannuation guidance notes to
  help superannuation fund trustees comply with the
  Superannuation Industry (Supervision) Act 1993.

- *Super Fund Lookup website <www.superfundlookup.
  gov.au>.* This is a free service that provides general
  information about superannuation funds that
  have an Australian business number (ABN). It
  will provide contact details and advise whether the
  fund is a complying superannuation fund that is

registered to accept superannuation contributions (for instance, employer superannuation guarantee contributions) and rollover payments. For more information see Super Fund Lookup Frequently Asked Questions (FAQ) on the website.

Professional service providers

If you know nothing about investing or you need personal advice about superannuation, a professional who holds an Australian Financial Service Licence (for instance, financial planners and certain accountants) can steer you in the right direction. All the major retail and industry super funds have financial planners if you need assistance. On the other hand, if you need taxation advice relating to superannuation issues, you can visit a recognised tax adviser and, more particularly, a registered tax agent. A tax agent is a person who is authorised to give you advice about managing your tax affairs, and they can prepare and lodge a superannuation tax return on your behalf. This is important to know if you plan to set up and manage an SMSF.

 Tax tip

Fees paid to obtain financial advice from a financial planner or tax advice from a registered tax agent are ordinarily a tax-deductible expense. But fees for drawing up an investment plan are considered to be capital in nature and they are not tax deductible.

Tax tip

If you want to check out whether you have any lost or unclaimed superannuation fund benefits, you can visit the Tax Office website <www.ato.gov.au> and use the superannuation tool SuperSeeker. To do this search you will need to provide your TFN, family and given names, and date of birth.

Tax tip

The Tax Office maintains a special account called Superannuation Holding Accounts Reserve (SHAR). This account holds small unclaimed employer super guarantee payments and super co-contribution payments not yet transferred to member accounts. You can use the Tax Office search tool SuperSeeker to check if you have any unclaimed benefits in this account. For more details see the Tax Office publication *Superannuation holding accounts (SHA) special account*.

Useful references

- Superannuation information <www.australia.gov.au>, go to 'Superannuation'

- Australia's Superannuation System <www.supersystemreview.gov.au>

- Australian Securities & Investments Commission (ASIC) consumer website <www.moneysmart. gov.au>. Go to 'About financial products', then 'Superannuation'

- Australian Government Employees Superannuation Trust (AGEST) website <www.agest.com.au>

- Seniors information website <www.seniors.gov.au>, 'The online source for all Australians over 50'

Australian Taxation Office publications

- *All super funds must lodge income tax returns*

- *Changes to super*

- *Choosing a super fund – How to complete your standard choice form*

- *Guide to superannuation for individuals*

- *Key superannuation rates and thresholds*

- *New SMSF member verification system*

- *Salary sacrificing super*

- *Searching for lost super* (NAT 2476)

- *Super for same-sex couples and their children (individuals)*

- *Super terms explained*

- *Superannuation and unclaimed super*

- *Superannuation spouse contribution tax offset*

- *Superannuation tips for young people*
- *Turning 60—what does it mean for super fund members?*

Other taxation rulings

- SGR 2009/2: *Superannuation guarantee: meaning of the terms 'ordinary time earnings' and 'salary or wages'*

Chapter 2

Long-term commitment: how much you need to accumulate

The federal government introduced compulsory superannuation in the 1990s. This move sent the message that all Australians have to plan for their own retirement. Relying on the age pension to subsidise your lifestyle in retirement is no longer a viable option, unless you can meet certain conditions. To qualify for the age pension you need to satisfy a residency test and a strict income test and asset test. These tests are to check whether the total income you derive each year and the amount of assets you currently own fall within acceptable limits. To make access to the age pension even more difficult, the federal government has legislated to progressively increase the age pension age to 67 years by 2023. In this chapter I discuss how much you need to accumulate to fund your retirement.

It's not your money until you retire

A major nuisance with contributing money into a complying superannuation fund is your inability to access your preserved benefits to help finance your immediate lifestyle needs. This could become a major concern if you need funds now (for instance, you want to buy a home), and you have a substantial sum locked away in your super fund that you can't touch. Unfortunately, superannuation is not like a bank account where you can make regular deposits and withdrawals. Technically speaking, any money you contribute to a super fund cannot be legally accessed until you reach your preservation age, and satisfy a condition of release (see chapter 8, and more particularly table 8.1 on p. 170). And there are stiff civil and criminal penalties to deter you from trying to do so!

Table 8.1 shows that if you were born before 1960 your preservation age is 55 years of age, and if you were born after 1964, your preservation age is 60. Depending on your age at the time you make a super contribution, you may need to wait for more than 40 years before you can access your preserved benefits.

How much should you put into super each year?

Ideally, the earlier you start and the more you contribute to your super fund each year; the greater the benefits you can expect to have when you decide to hang up the pen or shovel. Unfortunately, not everyone is in a position to contribute a substantial sum each year. The amount you can afford will usually depend on your current age, your gross annual salary and your personal circumstances. As superannuation is a long-term retirement strategy, it's best to plan well ahead and choose an appropriate investment option in your super fund, or appropriate investments if you have an SMSF, that have the capacity to deliver long-term capital growth (see chapter 7).

Many superannuation funds provide free retirement calculators on their websites, which you can use to help you work out how much you need to set aside each week, and how long it will take to accrue the amount you require. These retirement calculators take into account the following key variables:

- your current age

- your gross annual salary

- your intended retirement age

- your current superannuation balance

- whether you intend to salary sacrifice (make before-tax contributions deducted from your salary)

- whether you intend to make personal non-concessional (after-tax) contributions

- your super fund's investment earnings rate

- your super fund's fees and charges.

 Tax trap

There are statutory provisions to restrict the amount you can contribute to a complying super fund each year, and you must comply with these limits. And if you breach these rules, the excess amount you contribute is liable to tax at the rate of 46.5 per cent. You can only build up your benefits within these limitations (see chapter 5).

Young adults and superannuation

If you have just completed full-time education and you're in your early twenties, retirement is not likely to be a major priority at this point in your life, given that you need to wait more than 40 years before you can access your super. However, under current legislation, once you turn 18 years of age and earn more than $450 per month, your employer must make superannuation guarantee contributions on your behalf to your nominated super fund. The contribution rate is currently 9 per cent of your gross salary. For instance, if you're currently earning $600 a week; your employer will contribute $54 to your nominated super fund ($600 × 9 per cent = $54).

Of course, the more you earn, the greater the contribution being made on your behalf. The federal government plans to progressively increase the super guarantee contribution rate to 12 per cent by 2019–20; see appendix A, table 11.

If you have some surplus funds, you have the option to make salary sacrifice contributions or non-concessional contributions (after-tax contributions) to your super fund as well. Under a salary sacrifice arrangement, extra super contributions are deducted from your gross salary or pre-tax income (see chapter 5). If you earn less than $31 920, you could take advantage of the federal government's superannuation co-contribution scheme. Under this plan, if you make a $1000 non-concessional contribution (or after-tax contribution), the federal government will contribute $1000 to your super fund as well (which is effectively a 100 per cent return on your investment!). But, as they say in the small print, conditions apply (see chapter 5).

At a glance: super and low-income earners

The federal government has introduced a number of tax incentives to help low-income earners boost their retirement savings. These include the following.

- If you earn less than $37 000, the federal government intends to contribute up to $500 to your account to eliminate the effect of any contributions tax that's payable on your employer's superannuation guarantee contributions.

■ If your assessable income is less than $31 920, and you make a $1000 non-concessional (after-tax) contribution to your super fund, the federal government will make a $1000 contribution on your behalf. The amount the government contributes reduces if you earn more than $31 920 and ceases once you earn more than $61 920; see appendix A, table 10.

Maturing nicely

So you have reached your mid forties and have an established and well-paid job. In this case, salary sacrificing a sizeable portion of your gross salary may be high on your to-do list. This is especially the case if your current superannuation fund balance is nothing to write home about. If you do this, your combined employer and employee contributions cannot exceed the concessional contribution cap amount. This is currently $25 000 if you're under 50 years of age. For example, if your gross annual salary is $80 000, your employer is required to make a $7200 super guarantee contribution on your behalf ($80 000 × 9 per cent = $7200). Under these circumstances, the most you can salary sacrifice is limited to $17 800 ($25 000 − $7200 = $17 800). But you can make non-concessional (after-tax) contributions as well (see chapter 5 for more details).

Approaching retirement age

One great thing about superannuation is your capacity to substantially boost the amount you can contribute each year to a complying super fund. If you can afford to do so, making a sizeable payment may be worth contemplating if you're close to your preservation age and you're keen to maximise your retirement benefits (see Case study: funding your pension on p. 196). For instance, if you're in your mid fifties, in addition to making a $50 000 concessional (before-tax) contribution, you can also make a one-off $450 000 non-concessional (after-tax) contribution. If you make a $450 000 non-concessional contribution, you can't make any further non-concessional contributions for the next two years (see chapter 5). You can also take advantage of contribution splitting, which allows you to split any concessional contributions you make to your super fund with your spouse or partner.

 Tax tip

From 1 July 2012 if you're over 50 years of age, the maximum concessional contribution you can make to a complying super fund reduces from $50 000 to $25 000 per year. However, the federal government has proposed that you will still be able to make a $50 000 concessional contribution each year if you have less than $500 000 in your super fund account.

Let the good times roll: income in retirement

The level of income you need to live in retirement depends mainly on the lifestyle you want in your old age, as well as on your current life expectancy. For instance, a person aged 60 is likely to live for another 25 years in retirement. When calculating how much capital you need to accrue, you need to take into account issues such as the impact of inflation, and the possibility that you could run out of money if you were to live to a ripe old age. A qualified financial planner can help you with this exercise. Currently it's generally considered a single person needs around $40 000 of income each year for a comfortable lifestyle, while a couple needs around $54 000 for a comfortable lifestyle in their old age. For more information see *Westpac ASFA Retirement Standard* on the ASFA website <www.superannuation.asn.au> (to find the details, click on 'Resource Centre' on the home page and choose 'Retirement Standard' from the drop-down menu).

As a general guide, 70 per cent of your final average salary is ordinarily regarded as a reasonable pension for maintaining a comfortable lifestyle in retirement. If you accept this point of view, the capital you need to accumulate is about 15 times your desired pension. So, according to this formula, if you consider $60 000 to be a reasonable pension per year, you need to accumulate around $900 000 by the time you call it a day and retire ($60 000 × 15 = $900 000). Once you have determined the amount of capital you need, it then becomes a simple matter of calculating the amount you must contribute each year, the likely investment earnings rate of the fund, minus income tax and account-keeping fees. Using a retirement calculator can help you with this exercise.

Tax tip

If you find your super fund pension is minimal, you may be eligible to receive certain government top-up payments from Centrelink, such as the age pension. You need to satisfy an income test and an asset test to get an age pension. These tests check whether your income and assets are within acceptable limits. A financial planner can help you with this matter. The age pension is ordinarily treated as assessable income. However, when you take into account the various tax offsets you may qualify for, such as a low-income tax offset and the senior Australians tax offset, the amount of tax payable may be reduced to nil; see appendix A, table 4. For more details, visit the Centrelink website <www.centrelink.gov.au>.

And it's all tax free!

A significant benefit of being a member of a super fund is that, once you turn 60 years of age and satisfy a condition of release (such as retiring) all pensions and lump sum payments payable from super funds are exempt from tax. Both a lump sum and a pension are also excluded from your assessable income! So as far as the Tax Office is concerned, if your super pension is your sole source of income, your taxable income is effectively nil. This is great news if you also derive assessable income from other sources (such as interest, dividends and rent). This is because, under Australian tax law, no tax is payable once your taxable income falls below \$16 000, given that you can claim a low-income tax offset; see appendix A, table 3. The good news gets even better, because once you turn 65 years of age you could also qualify for a senior Australians tax offset; see appendix A, table 4. To add icing to the retirement cake, the investment earnings your fund derives to fund your pension payments is also exempt from tax. For example, if you had managed to accumulate \$900 000 in your super fund, and the fund's investment earning rate is 8 per cent per year, \$72 000 will be credited to your account each year, and no tax is payable on this amount (\$900 000 × 8 per cent = \$72 000).

Useful references

- Understanding Money website <www.understandingmoney.gov.au>, and click on 'Superannuation' and 'Retirement'.

- Australian Securities & Investments Commission consumer website <www.moneysmart.gov.au>, go to:

  - 'Tools and resources' and click on 'Calculators and tools' from the drop-down menu, and 'Superannuation calculator' from the page that opens

  - 'About you' and choose 'Young adults' from the drop-down menu, and 'Top 10 finance tips for young people' from the page that opens

- Centrelink website <www.centrelink.gov.au>. Go to 'Individuals', then 'Retirement' and click on 'Age pension' under the heading 'Payments'

Australian Taxation Office publications

- *Superannuation tips for young people*

Chapter 3

Setting up a self managed super fund: the good, the bad and the ugly

A self managed superannuation fund (SMSF) is worth contemplating if you run your own business or you're in your mid forties and have an existing superannuation fund with an accumulated balance of more than $250 000. Although you can gain significant benefits from managing your own fund, like all good things in life, it comes at a cost. There are strict rules and regulations you must obey, and stiff financial penalties apply if you contravene them. So it's best to familiarise yourself with these statutory provisions before you commit yourself. If you're not sure what to do, you should seek advice from professionals who hold an Australian Financial Service Licence (such as financial planners and certain accountants). In this chapter, I discuss how to establish an SMSF, and the benefits and limitations of running the show yourself.

Do-it-yourself super funds

The *Income Tax Assessment Act* permits individuals to set up and manage their own superannuation funds. According to the Tax Office, SMSFs are now the largest and fastest growing segment of the superannuation industry. There are currently around 440000 SMSFs in existence, and the number of SMSF members is estimated to be around 820000 (which is great news if you happen to be a tax consultant or person who specialises in auditing SMSFs).

An SMSF is defined as a fund with fewer than five members, which means that you can have only a maximum of four members in your fund. You also need to comply with a number of technical rules. The main ones are listed here:

- Each individual member of your fund must be made a trustee (or director if you have a corporate trustee for your fund). You need to do this because an SMSF is technically a trust.

- All the members need to be aware of their statutory duties and responsibilities with respect to managing an SMSF (and ignorance of the law is no excuse).

- No member can be an employee of another member unless they are related.

- Trustees cannot be remunerated for their services. However, according to Tax Office Ruling Self Managed Superannuation Funds Ruling (SMSFR) 2008/2: 'trustees may reimburse themselves or pay out of the trust property expenses that have been properly incurred in the performance of those duties'; see also appendix B, Reimbursement of expenses incurred by trustees.

 Tax tip

Special rules apply if you want to set up a single member fund. You can run a single member SMSF provided you have another trustee who is either a relative or person who is not employed by you. Alternatively, if you have a corporate trustee for your single member fund, you will need to be one of the directors, and you will need to have another director who is either a relative or person who is not employed by you.

Generally the members who run an SMSF normally have a family relationship (for instance, husband, wife and children) or are close friends. The members of an SMSF can also include business partners.

At a glance: benefits of running your own fund

Some of the benefits you can gain from running an SMSF are listed overleaf.

- You can manage and control your own super fund.

- You can select the investments to help fund your retirement, such as real estate, shares listed on the Australian Securities Exchange, and managed funds (see chapter 7).

- An SMSF can own rental properties, and after you turn 60 years of age, any capital gains you make on the sale of rental properties during the pension phase is tax free (see chapter 8).

- You can make personal superannuation contributions to your SMSF.

- An SMSF can receive employer superannuation guarantee contributions.

- An SMSF can purchase your business premises and lease it back to you (see chapter 4).

- An SMSF is concessionally taxed at the rate of 15 per cent, and it's possible for your fund to pay no tax if it receives dividend franking credits (see chapter 6).

- You can transfer listed securities (for instance, your share portfolio) to your super fund. But you could be liable to pay capital gains tax if you make a capital gain at the time of transfer; as there will be a change in ownership (see chapter 4).

- You can roll over (transfer) benefits you have in other super funds into your SMSF (see chapter 5).

- An SMSF can pay you a tax-free pension after you turn 60 years of age and retire, or it can pay a transition to retirement pension once you turn 55 years of age (see chapter 8).

- You can outsource administrative duties to superannuation fund specialists.

- You can instigate estate planning strategies.

- An SMSF can take out life insurance on behalf of its members and the premiums payable are tax deductible.

 Tax tip

If you want your employer to pay superannuation guarantee contributions into your SMSF, you need to supply a copy of documentation from the Tax Office confirming that your SMSF had made an election to be regulated—for more details see the Tax Office publication *Choosing a super fund: how to complete your Standard choice form* (NAT 13080). You can download a copy from the Tax Office website <www.ato.gov.au>.

Although these benefits may look appealing, you need to weigh up whether you have the necessary investment skills and commitment to manage and run a complying super fund. The bad news is that stiff penalties apply if you contravene the *Superannuation Industry (Supervision) Act 1993* (SIS Act), so it's important that you know your duties and responsibilities. A key test of whether it's a good idea to operate your own fund is whether you can outperform the professionally managed industry funds and retail funds. Furthermore, you will incur ongoing running costs, such as accounting and audit fees, and an annual $180 supervisory levy (see chapter 6). The amount of fees you pay each year will depend primarily on whether you outsource the administrative duties to super fund specialists, the category of investments your fund holds, and whether you intend to have individual trustees or corporate trustees operate your fund. But the good news here is these outlays are ordinarily a tax-deductible expense.

At a glance: what you can't do in an SMSF

Members of an SMSF are prohibited from the following:

- acquiring property from a related party (for instance, from a member or member's relative)

- residing in a residential property that is owned by your SMSF

- enjoying a direct or indirect benefit from your super fund's investment holdings; for instance, you can't display works of art your super fund owns in your place of residence or wear jewellery your super fund may own as an investment asset

- benefiting from using shareholder discount cards that companies may offer their shareholders

- using your super fund's assets as a guarantee to secure a personal loan

- selling SMSF assets and providing financial assistance to a member to pay off debts that a member may personally owe; see appendix B, Financial assistance to members

- lending money to a member or to a member's relative, such as a spouse, child or parent; this could become a major dilemma if you need money urgently and you have substantial investment assets sitting in your super that you can't access

- carrying on a business as an SMSF, as the sole purpose of running a super fund must be to provide retirement benefits or benefits to dependants in the event of a member's death.

 Tax trap

If a member of your SMSF were to reside overseas for an extended period (for instance, more than two years), there's a risk your SMSF could be classified as a non-resident fund and be taxed as a non-complying super fund. To minimise the risk, contact the Tax Office before you go or seek professional advice from a licensed professional. For more details see the Tax Office publication *Residency of self managed super funds* and Tax Office Ruling TR 2008/9. See also appendix B, Residency test (self managed super funds).

Getting started: the steps you need to complete

Setting up an SMSF is relatively straightforward. For an initial outlay of around $1000 you can buy a ready made complying superannuation fund package that sets out the various steps you need to follow; including all the legal paperwork you have to complete and sign. Your accountant or tax agent can help you get hold of a complying super fund package tailored to meet your particular circumstances. See also the Tax Office publication *Setting up a self managed super fund* (NAT 71923).

The key steps and documents you need to attend to when establishing an SMSF are listed here.

Trust deed

You need to sign a properly drafted superannuation fund trust deed. This legal document sets out the governing rules your fund must comply with in order to qualify for certain tax concessions. A trust deed is essential to prove that you have a genuine SMSF. The trust deed will set out the following important rules.

Fund's objectives

The sole purpose of setting up an SMSF must be to provide benefits to members upon retirement, and to dependants in the event of a member's death.

Appointment of trustees

Because an SMSF is a trust, the trust deed must specify how to appoint (and remove) trustees. It will also set out your intention to appoint a corporate trustee (corporate basis) or individual trustee (pension basis) to manage and run your super fund. The duties and responsibilities of the trustee under each option are similar. If you have a corporate trustee, you can make a lump sum payment or pension on retirement. On the other hand, if you have an individual trustee, the sole purpose of running the fund is to pay a pension. But in this case you also have discretion to commute (change) the payment into a lump sum. You need to weigh up the administrative costs, and legal advantages and limitations regarding each option. Discuss this matter with your super fund provider at the time you set up the fund. Incidentally, all the members of your SMSF must be trustees (or directors if you decide to have a corporate trustee).

Powers of trustees

The duties and responsibilities of trustees, such as lodging an annual super fund tax return, and appointing an approved auditor to check that the fund is a complying fund, must be set out in the trust deed. The Tax Office expects all members to be aware of all the stringent rules and regulations associated with running an SMSF. It also expects that you do not contravene the sole purpose test (per superannuation Tax Office Ruling SMSFR 2007/D1).

According to the Tax Office *Self managed super fund trustee declaration form—trustee duties*, an individual trustee or director of the corporate trustee must:

- act honestly in all matters concerning the fund

- exercise skill, care and diligence in managing the fund

- act in the best interests of all the members of the fund.

Member application

This clause sets out who can be a member of your SMSF, such as members of your immediate family.

Contributions

The rules for making a contribution to your super fund must be in accordance with the *Income Tax Assessment Act 1997* (see figure 5.1 on p. 85). All the members of your fund will need to provide their individual tax file numbers (TFNs) at the time the fund is established. Everyone needs to do this before your super fund can accept member contributions.

Payment of benefits to members

This section sets out how benefits are to be paid when a member meets a certain condition of release (such as the payment of pensions or lump sum cash withdrawals, or a combination of the two—see chapter 8).

Winding up fund

This sets out the procedures you need to follow if you wind up your SMSF.

Election to be regulated

You must lodge an election to become a regulated SMSF under the *Superannuation Industry (Supervision) Act 1993* (SIS Act). This election is irrevocable: you can't change your decision at a later date. You need to do this within 60 days of setting up the fund. For more details, see the Tax Office publication *How your self-managed super fund is regulated* (NAT 71454).

Tax file number (TFN)

Your TFN is your superannuation fund identification number. You will ordinarily be issued a TFN at the time you make an election to be regulated. You need to quote this number when you lodge your *Self managed superannuation fund annual return*.

Australian business number (ABN)

You may need to quote your Australian business number (ABN) if your super fund enters into certain financial transactions. You will ordinarily be issued an ABN at the time you make an election to be regulated. The ABN is used by employers and other super funds to check on the federal government Super Fund Lookup website

<www.superfundlookup.gov.au> which shows whether your fund is a complying fund, and whether it can accept super contributions and rollover payments (see chapter 1).

Trustee declarations

All super fund members must sign a trustee declaration form to certify that they consent to be trustees. You need to do this within 21 days of becoming a trustee or director. There is a further requirement that all trustees need to be aware of their legal duties and responsibilities. You can't be a trustee if you're a 'disqualified person' (for instance, an undischarged bankrupt or person convicted for dishonesty) or if you're under 18 years of age. For more details see the Tax Office publication *Trustee declaration* (NAT 71099).

Investment strategy document

You need to formulate an investment strategy for your SMSF, setting out the types of investments you intend to consider to help build member benefits (see Investment strategy in chapters 4 and 6).

Bank account

You need to open a superannuation fund bank account (in the name of the fund) in order to make cash contributions (or roll over, or transfer, money from other funds you may belong to into your SMSF), and meet any expenses or liabilities your fund may incur.

The Tax Office has advised that the fund's assets should be held in a legally recognised ownership arrangement, for instance:

- in the names of all of the individual trustees as trustees of your fund

- in the name of the company as trustee for your fund in the case of a corporate trustee.

Membership application form

You will need to provide a membership application form which members will need to complete when they join the fund. A disqualified person cannot be a member of an SMSF, and the member must be an Australian resident.

GST registration

Under certain circumstances your super fund may need to register for goods and services tax (GST), for instance if your super fund owns a commercial property and receives rent that exceeds $75 000 per year. If you register for GST your super fund can claim a GST credit in respect of any GST payments the fund may incur in administering the fund. The GST credit is limited to 75 per cent of the GST payment.

Binding death benefit nomination forms

It is recommended that you provide binding death benefit nomination forms for members to nominate their beneficiaries—who should receive their super in the event of the member's death. Members need to complete a binding death benefit nomination form if they want their benefits to be paid to a specific dependant (or to your estate) in the event of your death (see chapter 1). If you plan to make a binding nomination, make sure you follow all the proper legal procedures in accordance with the trust deed. Legal disputes can arise if your instructions are not clear and precise; see appendix B, Self managed superannuation funds (and death benefit payments).

Estate planning

Your fund needs to know how to deal with member benefits in the event of a member's death. When dealing with legal issues (and to avoid potential legal disputes), it's best that you discuss this matter with a solicitor at the time you set up the fund. For a discussion on estate planning issues, visit the Australian Government website <www. seniors.gov.au> and go to 'Estate planning'.

Insurance cover

It's recommended that each member should consider taking out adequate life insurance cover in the event of death or disability. Death and disability premiums payable by a complying super fund are a tax-deductible expense (see chapter 6).

Record keeping

You need to establish a proper recording system to record minutes of trustee meetings, the receipt of member contributions, and the fund's earnings and expenditure. You also need to keep separate accounts for each member to record their member benefits. Your accountant can help you with this exercise. There are also numerous accounting software packages that can do all of this for you. You can find them on the internet: key search words are superannuation accounting software packages.

Transfer forms

To transfer any benefits you have in other super funds into your SMSF, you will need to fill in the form *Completing the request to transfer whole balance of superannuation benefits between funds* (NAT 71223).

Administration

The trustees of the SMSF can appoint service providers, such as an accountant, to administer the fund and an approved auditor to check that you're not contravening the SIS Act. If you breach any provisions the auditor must report the contraventions to the Tax Office. The auditor must be an independent auditor (meaning they can't be the same person who prepared your accounts). An audit must be done each financial year, and before you lodge your super fund's annual tax return (see chapter 4).

Tax tip

According to Tax Office Ruling IT 2672, costs incurred by a trustee of a superannuation fund in amending a trust deed are tax deductible if the amendments are necessitated by changes in government regulations, and are made to ensure that the fund's day-to-day operations continue to satisfy the Insurance and Superannuation Commission's (ISC) requirements for a complying superannuation fund.

Tax tip

According to Tax Office Ruling IT 2672, costs incurred in establishing a trust, executing a new deed for an existing fund, and amending a deed to enlarge or significantly alter the scope of the trust's activities are *not* tax deductible.

Useful references
Australian Taxation Office publications

- *GST and financial supplies for self-managed super funds* (NAT 71512)

- *Is self-managed super right for you?* (NAT 13556)

- *Keeping good records*

- *Request for self-managed superannuation fund specific advice (NAT 72441)*

- *Running a self-managed super fund* (NAT 11032)

- *Self-managed super funds — setting up a self-managed super fund* (NAT 71923)

- *Thinking about self-managed super* (NAT 72579)

- *Winding up a self-managed super fund* (NAT 8107)

- *Your trust deed*

Chapter 4

Running a self managed super fund: the rules you have to follow

Once you set up a self managed super fund (SMSF) and lodge an election to be regulated, you need to comply with all the rules and regulations set out in the *Superannuation Industry (Supervision) Act 1993* (SIS Act). If you contravene those rules, your SMSF could be made non-compliant, and you would lose all the tax benefits that super normally offers. So it's best that you understand what you must do at the outset. In this chapter, I'll talk about the major statutory provisions you need to comply with if you want to run an SMSF.

At a glance: common mistakes with SMSFs

The Tax Office has identified the following common mistakes associated with running an SMSF.

Tax returns

- overstating super fund tax deductions

- incorrectly claiming tax deductions

- not lodging an SMSF annual tax return on time

- refusing to lodge an SMSF tax return.

Contributions

- making non-cash contributions (such as listed securities and business real property) to your fund and not recording the transactions at their true market value (Taxpayer Alert TA 2008/12)

- incorrectly receiving contributions from members over the age of 65 who have failed a work test—once a member turns 65 they can't make a contribution unless they work a minimum of 40 hours over 30 consecutive days in the year in which they make the contribution.

Accumulation phase

- failing the definition of an Australian superannuation fund as set out in Tax Office Ruling TR 2008/09

- failing to value the fund's assets at their market value at the end of the financial year

- recording the fund's assets in the name of the member—fund assets must be recorded under the fund's name

- incorrectly recording in-house assets and holding in-house assets that exceed 5 per cent of the market value of the fund's total assets

- gaining a benefit from your SMSF assets before you satisfy a condition of release (such as when you retire)

- making unauthorised loans from the fund to members and their relatives, and the fund receiving loans from members

- failing to provide relevant documents to the fund's auditor within 14 days of the auditor making such a request.

Pension phase

- failing to pay cash pensions to a member—a fund cannot make an in-specie, or non-cash, pension payment to a member

- making contributions to the fund pension account, rather than to an accumulation account, when the fund is in the pension phase

- being unable to convert pension assets to cash (for instance, property) to meet minimum pension payments to members

For more information, see the Tax Office publication *Self-managed superannuation fund: common mistakes and other compliance issues*. You can download a copy from the ATO website <www.ato.gov.au>.

Approved auditor

To keep you on the straight and narrow, the trustees of an SMSF must appoint an approved auditor each year to check that you're not cooking the books, and that your super fund is complying with the SIS Act. Your fund must be audited each year before the lodgement of your SMSF annual return. The auditor must provide an audit report to the trustees of your super fund and report any contraventions to the Tax Office. And this is all done at your fund's expense!

At a glance: what your auditor is checking

When your super fund is audited the auditor will check whether your fund:

- satisfies the definition of an SMSF (see chapter 3)

- has contravened the sole purpose test

- is lending or providing assistance to any member or relative of a member

- has acquired unauthorised assets from related parties

- has entered into any unauthorised borrowing

- has contravened the in-house asset rules

- is conducting investment transactions at arms length (see chapter 7)

- is keeping assets separate from personal assets the trustees may own

- has contravened the rules for accepting contributions from members (see chapter 5)

- has paid unauthorised benefits to members or their dependants (see chapter 8)

- is keeping proper records and, more particularly, has an investment strategy.

 Tax tip

The Tax Office has issued the publication *Approved auditors and self-managed super funds—role and responsibilities of approved auditors* (NAT 11375), which lists all the rules and regulations an SMSF must satisfy to become a complying super fund. This guide can help you to understand your duties and responsibilities, and what you need to do to ensure you don't contravene these provisions.

Tax trap

The Tax Office conducts routine tax audits and data-matching checks (where information disclosed in your super fund's tax return is matched with information obtained from various government agencies and external sources). This is to test whether the trustees are complying with all the provisions associated with running an SMSF. Financial penalties may apply, and your super fund could be made non-compliant. If the breaches are serious, you could face criminal prosecution.

Sole purpose test

An SMSF must be established and run for the sole purpose of providing benefits to members upon retirement, and benefits to dependants in the event of a member's death (core purpose), or provide benefits to members owing to physical or mental ill-health (ancillary purpose). These core purposes must be clearly set out in your super fund's trust deed (see chapter 3). The sole purpose test is also a key condition to be met if you choose to have individual trustees, and you want to pay pensions to members.

The sole purpose test effectively means that you can't gain any financial assistance, or benefit from using and enjoying the fund's assets, until you satisfy a condition of release (such as when you reach your preservation age and retire). If you breach this strict provision, the fund may lose its compliance status and all the tax concessions available to complying super funds. If you're made non-compliant the fund is liable to pay a 45 per cent tax rate, rather than the 15 per cent complying super funds pay. Depending on the seriousness of the contravention, trustees could be liable to fines and imprisonment. For more details, see Tax Office Ruling SMSFR 2008/2.

 Tax tip

The Tax Office has ruled that, under certain circumstances, a trustee of an SMSF can purchase a trauma insurance policy in respect of a member and still satisfy the sole purpose test. For more details see Tax Office Determination SMSFD 2010/1: *Self managed superannuation funds: the application of subsection 66(1) of the* Superannuation Industry (Supervision) Act 1993 to the acquisition of an asset by a self managed superannuation fund from a related party.

 Tax trap

A famous tax case relating to the sole purpose test is known as the Swiss Chalet case; see appendix B, Sole purpose test, case 43/95. The super fund contravened the sole purpose test when a member gained pre-retirement benefits from personally using and enjoying the fund's assets, which included units in a family trust that owned a Swiss chalet, a holiday home, and shares in a private

Tax trap *(cont'd)*

company that gave the member playing rights at a particular golf club. The fund's assets were also made available to family and friends. It goes without saying that the fund lost its compliant status and was subsequently taxed as a non-complying super fund for a number of years.

Loans and financial assistance to members

Although you may have a truckload of money sitting in your super fund that you're itching to get at, under the SIS Act trustees are prohibited from lending money or providing financial assistance to members, relatives or related parties. This is a common mistake associated with running an SMSF. Unfortunately, the money in your SMSF (just like the money you have in any super fund) is *not your money* until you satisfy a condition of release (see chapter 8). As the Tax Office considers the SMSF giving loans or financial assistance to members and related parties to be a serious breach, there are severe penalties if you contravene this important provision. Your super fund could be made non-compliant and the trustees could face criminal prosecution. A trustee can, however, make loans to a related party, provided the loans do not exceed 5 per cent of the fund's total assets (see In-house assets on p. 72). For the Tax Office views on this issue, see Tax Office Ruling SMSFR 2008/1.

See also appendix B, Financial assistance to members, and Self managed superannuation funds (illegal access to super benefits).

Acquiring assets from related parties

Ordinarily the SIS Act prohibits an SMSF from acquiring certain assets from related parties. This is basically an anti-avoidance provision to stop members from potentially manipulating the system by selling 'duds' to their super fund, and accessing cash before they retire. However, an SMSF is permitted to acquire certain approved assets at their market value from its members. This is on the condition that the decision is in accordance with the SMSF's investment strategy and does not contravene the sole purpose test (see Investment strategy on p. 76). The approved assets your super can acquire are:

- business real property

- listed securities

- in-house assets.

There's more information about each of these assets overleaf.

 Tax tip

According to Tax office Ruling SMSFR 2008/D2, an SMSF can acquire from a related party an approved asset 'that is partly purchased by, and partly

> **Tax tip** *(cont'd)*
>
> contributed to, the SMSF'. If you do this 'the sum of the purchase consideration and the amount recorded as the contribution component must be equal to the market value of the asset'.

Business real property

If you carry on a business, your SMSF can acquire your business premises (referred to as business real property) at its market value. You can either sell the premises to your super fund or make an in-specie contribution (or non-cash contribution). This contribution can be made on the condition that the property is used 'wholly and exclusively' to run your business activities. If you want to take advantage of this concession, you can sell or transfer up to 100 per cent of your business premises (for instance, your office, factory, farm or shop) to your super fund, and your fund can lease it back to you at a commercial rate of rent. The net rent your super fund derives is taxed at the rate of 15 per cent, and the rent you pay is a tax-deductible expense. Your intention that your super fund should own up to 100 per cent of your business real property must be in accordance with your super fund's investment strategy. For more information, read the Tax Office publications *What does business real property mean?* and Tax Office Ruling SMSFR 2009/1: *Self managed superannuation funds: business real property for the purposes of the*

Superannuation Industry (Supervision) Act 1993. You can download a copy of each publication from the Tax Office website <www.ato.gov.au>.

 Tax tip

If your SMSF does not have sufficient funds to buy your business real property from you, your fund can borrow money using a 'limited recourse borrowing' arrangement to finance the purchase. Alternatively, if you make an in-specie contribution (where you transfer your business real property to your SMSF), there are statutory limits on the amount of concessional and non-concessional contributions you can contribute to a super fund each financial year. Penalties apply if you breach these provisions (see chapter 5 for more details).

 Tax tip

Technically speaking, according to the Tax Office:

Business real property in relation to an entity is defined as meaning:

⇒ any freehold or leasehold interest of the entity in real property; or

⇒ any interest of the entity in Crown land, other than a leasehold interest, being an interest that

Tax tip *(cont'd)*

> is capable of assignment or transfer, where the real property is used wholly and exclusively in one or more businesses (whether carried on by the entity or not), but does not include any interest held in the capacity of beneficiary of a trust estate.

Under the capital gains tax (CGT) provisions, if you sell or transfer your business premises to your SMSF, you could be liable to pay CGT if you make a capital gain on disposal of the asset. This is because there will be a change in ownership, as your SMSF will now own your business premises. A significant benefit of your SMSF owning your business premises is that, if your super fund sells the property during the super fund's pension phase, and makes a capital gain on the sale, the entire amount is free of tax (see chapter 8).

If you sell or transfer your business premises to your super fund 12 months after you buy it, and you make a capital gain on disposal, only 50 per cent of the capital gain is taxable. The balance is exempt and is excluded from your assessable income. Further, if you carry on a small business you may qualify for relief from CGT under the CGT concessions for small business. Under Australian tax law you're considered to be carrying on a small business if your annual turnover (business takings) is less than $2 million, or if the net value of your business assets is less than $6 million. For more details see the Tax Office publication *Concessions for small business entities—overview* (NAT 71398).

 Tax trap

Depending on which state or territory you reside in, your super fund may be liable to pay stamp duty at the time you sell or transfer your business real property to your SMSF. But you may be eligible for concessions or exemptions if you satisfy certain conditions. For more details, visit your local state or territory government revenue office website.

Listed securities

Under the SIS Act a member is permitted to sell or transfer 'listed securities' to an SMSF, provided they are sold or transferred at their market value. The Tax Office has advised that listed securities can include investments, such as shares listed on the Australian Securities Exchange (ASX) or other approved stock exchanges, units, bonds, debentures, options, interests in managed investment schemes, or other securities listed on the ASX. It can also include assets, such as gold bullion. Your fund is permitted to borrow money under a limited recourse borrowing arrangement to purchase approved assets such as 'listed securities' from its members (see Limited recourse borrowing on p. 74).

The decision to acquire these investment assets must be in accordance with the SMSF's investment strategy, and must not contravene the sole purpose test. If you make an in-specie contribution, the amount you transfer cannot exceed the contributions limits for making concessional and non-concessional contributions (see chapter 5). Under the CGT provisions, if you sell or transfer your listed securities to your SMSF, you could be liable to pay CGT if you make a capital gain on disposal. This is because there will be a change in ownership, as your SMSF will now own the securities.

In-house assets

The trustees of an SMSF can invest in 'in-house assets' that involve a related party (such as fund members and their relatives, or a related trust of your fund). This is on the condition that the in-house assets do not exceed 5 per cent of the market value of your super fund's total assets. For example, if the market value of your super fund's total assets is $250 000, the in-house assets the fund can hold are limited to $12 500 ($250 000 × 5 per cent = $12 500). Civil penalties apply if you breach the 5 per cent limit at the end of the financial year, and if the contravention is severe (for instance, excessive loans have been made), there's a risk the Tax Office could issue a notice of non-compliance; see appendix B, Self managed superannuation funds (breach of in-house rules). The Tax Office has advised that incorrectly recording in-house assets and holding in-house assets that exceed 5 per cent of the market value of the fund's total assets are common mistakes with SMSFs. Your auditor must report any contraventions to the Tax Office.

Where the in-house assets of an SMSF exceed the 5 per cent limit, the SIS Act requires the trustee to develop a written plan to rectify the breach within 12 months (such as selling some in-house assets the fund owns). Appropriate action may need to be taken during periods where the market value of your super fund's total asset holdings, (for instance, shares listed on the Australian Securities Exchange) are significantly rising or falling in line with the prevailing market.

Business real property that's leased to a related party, and property owned as tenants in common (that's not subject to a lease with a related party), are excluded from the definition of an in-house asset.

At a glance: what defines an in-house asset

The SIS Act defines an in-house asset as:

- an asset of the fund that is a loan to, or an investment in, a related party of the fund

- an investment in a related trust of the fund

- an asset of the fund subject to a lease or lease arrangement between a trustee of the fund and a related party of the fund.

For more details about in-house assets see Tax Office Ruling SMSF 2009/4: *Self managed superannuation funds:*

the meaning of 'asset', 'loan', 'investment in', 'lease' and 'lease arrangement' in the definition of an 'in-house asset' in the Superannuation Industry (Supervision) Act 1993. As this area of tax law can be complicated, it's best to seek professional advice if your super fund holds a significant amount of assets and intends to hold in-house assets.

Borrowings

Trustees of an SMSF are permitted to borrow money under limited circumstances. For instance, your super fund can borrow money to pay benefits to members who satisfy a condition of release (maximum borrowing period 90 days), or to cover the settlement of security transactions (maximum borrowing period seven days). This is on the condition that the amount you borrow does not exceed 10 per cent of your fund's total assets.

Limited recourse borrowing

An SMSF can borrow money using a limited recourse borrowing arrangement (or instalment warrant), to buy certain approved assets, such as a residential property, commercial property (and more particularly your business premises), listed securities (such as shares) and artwork. You need to comply with strict conditions if you want to use this borrowing arrangement to buy an approved asset.

Expressed simply, under a limited recourse borrowing arrangement, the investment asset is held in trust, and ownership cannot transfer to your super fund until your fund makes the final instalment payment. Further, the loan must be structured on a limited recourse basis. This effectively means that, if your super fund is unable to pay off the loan, the lender has no right to claim against your super fund's other assets to recover any debts that are still outstanding. The lender's right to recover any shortfall is limited to the specific asset in question. In other words, the lender, rather than your super fund, will suffer any potential loss in the event of default. For more information see the Tax Office publications *Instalment warrants and super funds—questions and answers* and Taxpayer Alert TA 2008/5: *Certain borrowings by self-managed superannuation funds*.

 Tax trap

In Tax Office Interpretative Decision ID 2007/58, the Tax Office ruled a trustee of an SMSF that operated a margin account to purchase listed shares had contravened the SIS Act, as they had borrowed money and granted a charge over shares that are assets of the fund.

Separation of assets

The SIS Act requires the trustees of an SMSF to keep money and other assets of the SMSF separate from any personal money and assets of the trustees. This means you can't mix your personal investment holdings with your super fund's investment holdings. To avoid contravening this provision it's best that you maintain a separate superannuation fund bank account to record the fund's investment transactions. For more details, see the Tax Office's ID 2002/976: *Keeping assets of a self-managed superannuation fund separate from assets of other parties.*

Keep proper records

You must maintain a record of the minutes of trustee meetings. You also have to keep separate member accounts; determine each financial year the earnings of the super fund; and notify members of their account balances at regular intervals (for instance, every six months). You will need to keep your super fund records for 10 years. In chapter 3 I pointed out that you can use any of the numerous accounting software packages to do all this for you.

Investment strategy

The trustees of an SMSF must prepare and implement an investment strategy to help maximise member returns. All investment decisions must be done on a strictly commercial basis, and must comply with the SIS Act. Your investment strategy must be put in writing and should set out the following information:

- *The fund's objectives.* You must state what you plan to achieve from your investment activities to help maximise member benefits. Your objectives must be realistic and capable of achievement. For example, you might plan to achieve a rate of return that's 5 per cent above Australia's annual inflation rate.

- *Diversification.* This is the different types of asset classes you plan to hold to help you achieve the fund's objectives. Assets can range from traditional investments (such as term deposits, government bonds, shares, property and managed funds) to exotics (such as artwork, classic cars and jewellery; see chapter 7). Keep in mind the sole purpose in holding these assets must be to fund retirement strategies, and that you can't use or personally benefit from them until you satisfy a condition of release (such as when you reach your preservation age and retire).

- *Investment risk.* This is the risk associated with the various asset classes you plan to hold to help increase member benefits. Although there are no rules to say you can't choose just one asset class (for instance, put all your money in the share market), it's best that you consider the merits of diversification across asset classes, to reduce the risk of poor performance that could adversely affect member benefits.

- *Investment yield.* This is the likely return on the various asset classes you plan to hold, and whether they have the capability of delivering long-term capital growth (see chapter 7).

- *Liquidity.* Your fund needs to have a sufficient cash flow to discharge the fund's existing and prospective liabilities. This could become a major concern if your super fund's investment assets consist solely of property that is either currently vacant or can't be quickly sold to pay benefits to a member who has met a legitimate condition of release (for instance, retirement), or to a dependant in the event of a member's death.

Trustees must make sure that all investment decisions they make are in accordance with the investment strategy. And they must not contravene the SIS Act. You need to review your investment strategy at regular intervals and make any appropriate adjustments in the best interest of the members.

Documentary evidence and valuations

Trustees must maintain documentary evidence to verify the existence of SMSF assets (such as a holding statement for shares and a certificate of title for property), and keep independent appraisals of how they are valued. With respect to valuations, you need to value your share portfolio at their market value. As share prices are published daily, this should be a fairly straightforward exercise. On the other hand, if your super fund owns property, you need to value each property at its historical cost (and revalue each one at regular intervals to reflect 'fair value'). For more details about valuations of SMSF assets see Australian Taxation Office Self Managed Superannuation Funds Superannuation Circular 2003/1.

See also APRA letter to trustees 16 April 2009, *Valuation of unlisted asset—general principles for trustees*. You can download a copy from the Australian Prudential Regulation Authority (APRA) website <www.apra.gov. au>. You need to produce documentary evidence of your SMSF assets and provide records of how the valuations were determined when your super fund is audited each year by the approved auditor.

 Tax tip

According to the Tax Office, the SIS Act provides 'a defence to trustees against an action for loss or damage suffered as a result of the trustee making an investment. This defence is available where the trustee can show that the investment was made in accordance with an investment strategy formulated under the investment strategy covenant' (Australian Tax Office, *Self-managed superannuation fund—investment strategy and investment restrictions.*)

 Tax trap

The Tax Office has advised if your SMSF is 'running an active business as part of its investment strategy' it may indicate that the super fund has contravened the sole purpose test. This may be the case if your super fund were to carry on a share-trading business, for instance.

Members can choose to have a pooled investment strategy, where all member funds are pooled; or it could have an individual investment strategy by which each member can choose their own investment strategy to help fund their retirement. If you plan to have a pooled investment strategy, you need to know how the fund's earnings are to be allocated to each member's account, and when you need to do this exercise. If you're not sure what to do, it's best that you seek professional advice.

Useful references

- Australian Prudential Regulation Authority Superannuation Circular No. III.A.4: *The sole purpose test*

- Australian Securities & Investments Commission (ASIC) consumer website <www.moneysmart. gov.au>. Go to 'About financial products', choose 'Superannuation' and then 'Self-managed super'.

- Australian Securities Exchange (ASX) website <www.asx.com.au>. Go to 'Products', and choose 'SMSFs'.

- Self Managed Superannuation Funds Trustee Education Program website <www.smsftrustee. com>. This is a free online training tool prepared by CPA Australia, the Institute of Chartered Accountants in Australia, and the National Institute of Accountants to help trustees comply with the superannuation provisions.

Australian Taxation Office publications

- *Carrying on a business in a self-managed superannuation fund*

- *Completing the auditor/actuary contravention report* (NAT 11299)

- *Limited recourse borrowing arrangements by SMSF—questions and answers*

- *SMSF risk and issues with reporting*

- *Self-managed superannuation fund—investment strategy and investment restrictions*

- *Tax relief for investors in instalment warrants*

- *SMSF News*—a regular newsletter you can subscribe to for the latest news from the ATO and ASIC. Google 'SMSF news'.

Australian Taxation Office interpretative decisions

- ID 2010/169 *Self managed superannuation fund: limited recourse borrowing arrangement—refinancing*

- ID 2010/170 *Self managed superannuation fund: limited recourse borrowing arrangement—third party guarantee*

- ID 2010/172 *Self managed superannuation fund: limited recourse borrowing arrangement—joint investors*

- ID 2010/184 *Self managed superannuation fund: limited recourse borrowing arrangement—capitalisation of interest*

- ID 2010/185 *Self managed superannuation fund: limited recourse borrowing arrangement—charge*

Other taxation rulings

- SMSFR 2008/D2: *Self Managed Superannuation Funds: the application of subsection 66(1) of the* Superannuation Industry (Supervision) Act 1993 *to contributions of assets to a self managed superannuation fund by a related party of that fund*

- SMSFR 2009/2: *Self-Managed Superannuation Funds: the meaning of 'borrow money' or 'maintain an existing borrowing of money' for the purposes of section 67 of the* Superannuation Industry (Supervision) Act 1993

- TA 2010/3: *Non market value acquisition of shares or share options by a self-managed superannuation fund*

- TA 2010/5: *The use of an unrelated trust to circumvent superannuation lending restrictions*

CHAPTER 5

Building the nest egg: making a super contribution

Making a superannuation contribution to a complying superannuation fund is not a simple matter of crediting a sum of money to your account, as is the case if you deposit money into a bank savings account. When dealing with the *Income Tax Assessment Act 1997* and *Superannuation Industry (Supervision) Act 1993* (SIS Act), there are strict rules you need to comply with. And if you get it wrong, the Tax Office could impose stiff penalties. Furthermore, once you make a contribution, you cannot legally touch that money until you satisfy a condition of release. In this chapter, I discuss the key provisions for making a superannuation contribution and the tax issues you need to be aware of.

Making a contribution

The federal government has introduced a number of concessions to encourage you to make a contribution to a complying super fund or retirement savings account (RSA). Under Australian tax law any person who is under 65 years of age is eligible to make a superannuation contribution, and there is no employment test that you need to satisfy. But this is not the case once you reach 65 years of age, as then you need to be gainfully employed (described as satisfying a work test) before you can make a contribution.

You can make two types of contributions to a superannuation fund or RSA. They are referred to as concessional contributions and non-concessional contributions. You must also comply with statutory rules that limit (or cap) the amount of concessional and non-concessional contributions you can make to your super fund each financial year. If you exceed these limits, the excess amount is liable to a 46.5 per cent tax rate (see figure 5.1). Under Australian tax law, you will be considered to have made a superannuation contribution when it is received by your superannuation fund (following Tax Office Ruling TR 2009/D3, paragraph 19).

Concessional contributions

Concessional contributions (also described as personal pre-tax contributions) are contributions you make to a complying super fund that qualifies for a tax deduction.

Figure 5.1: making a contribution to a self managed super fund

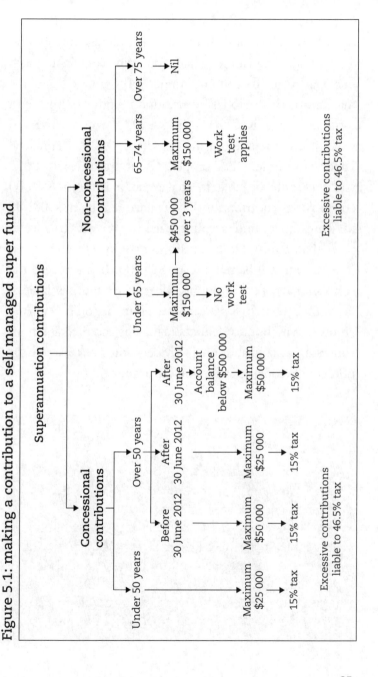

Concessional contributions are liable to 15 per cent contributions tax, and there is a concessional contribution cap amount to limit what you can contribute each financial year. If you are under 50 years of age the maximum concessional contribution you can make in a financial year is $25000 (indexed). If you are over 50 years of age, the amount increases to $50000. The federal Labor government has proposed that from 1 July 2012 you will only be able to make the maximum $50000 concessional contribution if you have less than $500000 in your super fund account balance. If your balance is more than $500000, the maximum you will be able to put in each year will be reduced to $25000. If you exceed the concessional contribution cap, the excess amount is liable to tax at the rate of 46.5 per cent (see figure 5.1 on p. 85). Any amount that's not tax deductible may be accepted as a non-concessional contribution (provided you don't exceed the non-concessional contribution cap amount).

 Tax trap

If you intend to make a concessional contribution to a complying super fund (or RSA), you need to provide your tax file number (TFN) to the trustee of your fund. If you fail to do this, your contributions are liable to be taxed at a rate of 46.5 per cent, rather than 15 per cent if you provide your TFN. If you supply your TFN to your fund at a later date (maximum three-year period), you can claim a no-TFN tax offset. If you do this, the additional tax you were charged is refunded to your account. For more details see the Tax Office publication *No tax file number (TFN) contributions.*

If you plan to make a concessional contribution and claim a tax deduction, you need to forward to your super fund a *Section 290-170 notice of intent to claim a deduction for personal super contributions*, and specify the amount you intend to claim. The trustee must acknowledge your notification and the amount you're claiming before you lodge your annual tax return. For more details see the Tax Office publication *Deduction for personal super contributions* (NAT 71121).

At a glance: what are concessional contributions?

The common types of concessional contribution are:

- employer super guarantee contributions made on behalf of employees

- employee salary sacrifice personal contributions

- personal pre-tax contributions by individuals who are self-employed or substantially self-employed and who qualify for a tax deduction.

Only employers and the self-employed (or substantially self-employed) can make concessional contributions. If you're an employee you can only make a non-concessional contribution; incidentally, the Tax Office classifies salary sacrifice contributions as employer super contributions—see Employee salary sacrifice personal contributions on p. 92).

 Tax tip

If you make a capital gain on sale of CGT assets (such as shares and property), you could consider making a personal contribution if the contribution qualifies for a tax deduction. If you do this, the amount you contribute can be deducted from the capital gain you made, and you could save a substantial amount of tax.

Employer super guarantee contributions

Under the superannuation guarantee legislation employers have a statutory obligation to make a superannuation contribution to a complying super fund on behalf of their employees. This will happen if you are an employee aged over 18 years and under 70 years, and earn more than $450 per month on either a full-time or part-time basis. The super guarantee rate is currently 9 per cent of your ordinary time earnings (or gross pay). For example, if you earn $1000 per week your employer must make a $90 super guarantee contribution to a complying super fund of your choice ($1000 × 9 per cent = $90) (see chapter 1). The federal Labor government has proposed to progressively increase the rate to 12 per cent by 2019–20; see appendix A, table 11.

Employers are not required to pay super guarantee contributions on employee salaries that exceed a statutory amount. For the 2010–11 financial year the statutory amount was $168 880; see appendix A, table 8.

A summary of your employer super guarantee contributions, and the date they were paid, is usually recorded on the member benefit statement that your super fund issues to you each year (see chapter 1). For more details see the Tax Office publication *Employer guide for reportable employer superannuation contributions.*

 Tax tip

You're considered to be an employee for the purposes of qualifying for an employer superannuation guarantee contribution if you're employed wholly or principally for your labour on a full-time, part-time or casual basis. For more details see the Tax Office publication *Superannuation Guarantee (SG) eligibility decision tool.*

Employers are statutorily obligated to make at least four super guarantee contributions to your super fund each year. The payments must be made no later than 28 days after the end of each quarter. The payments are ordinarily paid to your super fund within 14 days at the end of each month. If an employer fails to forward the super guarantee contributions to your super fund by the due date, the employer must prepare a *Superannuation guarantee statement* and pay the amount outstanding to the Tax Office. A super guarantee charge (or penalty) will apply, and the charge is not tax deductible. For more details see the Tax Office publication *Completing your superannuation guarantee charge statement—quarterly* (NAT 9600).

 Tax tip

If you run a small business and have fewer than 20 employees, the federal government has established a free superannuation clearing house service administered by Medicare Australia. This clearing house is to help fast track employer super guarantee contribution payments to the various super funds their employees may have nominated, as a consequence of the choice of super fund legislation. Employers who register for this service can pay their super guarantee contributions electronically to a single location. For more details see the Tax Office publication *Guide to superannuation for employers*.

 Tax tip

Employer contributions that are made on behalf of employees to a complying super fund are exempt from fringe benefits tax.

At a glance: who is not eligible for an employer super guarantee contribution

The following employees are not eligible for an employer super guarantee contribution:

- employees who earn less than $450 per month

- employees who are under 18 years of age and work 30 hours or fewer per week

- employees who are over 70 years of age (the federal Labor government proposes to increase the age limit from 70 to 75 from 1 July 2013)

- members of the Army, Navy or Air Force Reserve (the Tax Office has advised that the armed forces don't have to pay super contributions for reserve members)

- part-time nannies or housekeepers who are paid to do work of a domestic or private nature for fewer than 30 hours a week

- employees who earn salaries that exceed a statutory amount.

 Tax tip

Individual super fund members can split concessional contributions that were made in the previous financial year with their spouse. The maximum a member can split is 85 per cent of the

> **Tax tip** *(cont'd)*
>
> concessional contributions cap. You can split contributions that qualify for a tax deduction, such as employer contributions, salary sacrifice contributions and personal contributions. For more details about contributions splitting see the Tax Office publication *Contributions splitting* (NAT 15237) and more particularly the sections 'What contributions can be split?' and 'What contributions cannot be split?'.

Employee salary sacrifice personal contributions

To help build up the retirement nest egg, employees are permitted to make additional contributions under a salary sacrifice arrangement. Under this arrangement extra super contributions are deducted from your pre-tax gross pay. Unfortunately, employees can't claim a tax deduction for the additional amount they contribute, as they're ineligible to make a concessional contribution. But the trade-off here is that your salary or take home pay will reduce and you will pay less tax (see Case study: making a salary sacrifice contribution on p. 94). As the Tax Office classifies these additional contributions as employer super contributions, the amounts contributed are liable to 15 per cent contributions tax. If you decide to enter into a salary sacrifice agreement with your employer, the combined employer and employee contributions cannot exceed the concessional contribution cap amount. For example, if you're under 50 years of age the concessional contribution cap amount is $25 000. Under these circumstances, if your employer makes a $10 000 super guarantee contribution on your behalf, the most you can contribute under a salary sacrifice arrangement is $15 000 ($25 000 − $10 000 = $15 000).

Tax tip

For a comprehensive discussion about salary sacrifice arrangements and superannuation you can read Tax Office Ruling TR 2001/10: *Income tax: fringe benefits tax and superannuation guarantee: salary sacrifice arrangements.* You can download a copy from the Tax Office website <www.ato.gov.au>.

Tax trap

When you salary sacrifice you are effectively reducing your gross salary and taxable income. If you do this, your employer may recalculate the employer super guarantee contribution on your gross salary *less* the amount you salary sacrifice. For example, if your gross weekly salary is $1500 and you salary sacrifice $500, your employer may recalculate the employer super guarantee contribution on the lower amount, namely $1000 rather than $1500. It's best that you check this out with your employer when you enter into a salary sacrifice arrangement.

Case study: making a salary sacrifice contribution

Elise is a secondary school teacher earning a $75 000 salary. Under a salary sacrifice arrangement, her employer deducted a further $10 000 super contribution from her salary and paid the amount to her nominated super fund. When her employer did this, her gross salary was reduced from $75 000 to $65 000. As the Tax Office classifies these additional payments as employer super contributions, the $10 000 is liable to 15 per cent contributions tax. As the $10 000 would have been liable to tax at the rate of 31.5 per cent if Elise did not salary sacrifice, she will effectively save $1650 in tax: $10 000 × 31.5 per cent – 15 per cent = $1650. But the trade-off here is she cannot access these funds until she reaches her preservation age and satisfies a condition of release. Under the salary sacrifice arrangement, her employer agreed to calculate the employer superannuation contribution based on a salary of $75 000 rather than on the lower amount of $65 000.

Personal pre-tax contributions (non-concessional contributions)

A personal contribution, or non-concessional contribution, is a voluntary contribution that you can make to a complying super fund, but it doesn't qualify for a tax deduction. This is a good way of saving for your retirement given that investment earnings will be exempt from tax during the pension phase (see chapter 8). If you want to do this, you need to complete an application form and quote your TFN, and forward the details to your super fund. These contributions are not liable to 15 per cent contributions tax, as is the case if you make a concessional contribution.

Anyone who is under 65 years of age can make a personal or non-concessional contribution. But once you turn 65, you need to satisfy a work test, if you want to make a non-concessional contribution. To satisfy the work test, you need to work a minimum 40 hours over a 30-day consecutive period in the financial year in which you want to make the super contribution. Once you reach 75 years of age, you can no longer make a non-concessional contribution (see figure 5.1 on p. 85).

As is the case with concessional contributions, there is a non-concessional cap amount to limit the amount you can contribute each financial year. If you're under 65 years of age the non-concessional cap amount is $150000 each financial year (though this amount is indexed and increases regularly). Alternatively, if you're less than 65 years of age, you can make non-concessional contributions of up to a maximum $450000 during the financial year—this is referred to as the bring-forward option. If you make the maximum contribution, you can't make any further non-concessional contributions for the next two years. Once you turn 65 years of age, the maximum amount you can contribute each year is $150000, provided you satisfy the work test and are aged less than 75. If you exceed the non-concessional cap amount, the excess is liable to tax at the rate of 46.5 per cent (see figure 5.1 on p. 85).

Tax tip

It's possible for you to make a $600 000 non-concessional contribution over a short period of time. For instance, you can make a $150 000 non-concessional contribution just before the end of the financial year (for instance, in June), and a further $450 000 at the beginning of the next financial year (for instance, in July). This may be worth doing if you're close to 65 years of age and you're keen to boost the balance in your superannuation fund before restrictions are imposed.

Tax trap

An individual is not allowed to split non-concessional contributions and federal government co-contributions with their spouse. Different rules apply with concessional contributions.

Federal government concessions

The federal government has introduced a number of tax concessions to encourage low-income earners to make a contribution to a complying superannuation fund (see figure 5.2, overleaf). This is to help boost benefits that they can access when they retire. These concessions are:

- superannuation co-contribution scheme
- spouse contribution tax offset.

 Tax tip

The federal Labor government has proposed that, from 1 July 2013 if you earn less than $37000 and a concessional contribution is made to a complying super fund on your behalf, the federal government will contribute up to $500 to your fund account. This is to offset the 15 per cent contributions tax that's payable on concessional contributions that you make to a complying super fund.

Superannuation co-contribution scheme

If your total income is less than $31920 and you make a maximum $1000 personal after-tax non-concessional contribution to a complying super fund (or RSA), the federal government (through the Tax Office) will make a $1000 superannuation co-contribution payment on your behalf to your nominated super fund. The payment is reduced if you contribute less than $1000. On the other hand, if your total income is more than $31920, and you make a non-concessional contribution, the co-contribution payment reduces by 3.333 cents for every dollar you earn above $31920.

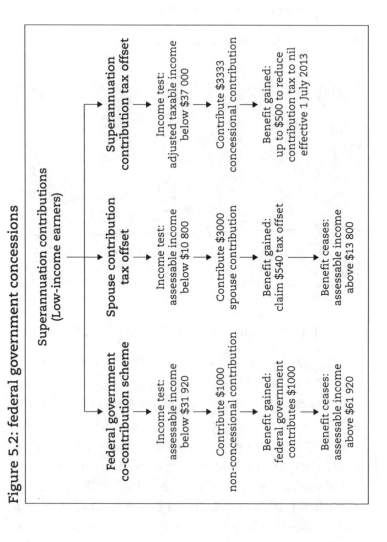

Figure 5.2: federal government concessions

Co-contributions cut out once your total income exceeds $61 920. You can use your super fund's online calculator to work out how much you're entitled to receive if you earn more than $31 920 (or you can use the Tax Office Super co-contribution calculator on its website at <www.ato.gov.au>). As you can do this each year, this could prove a great way of boosting your retirement benefits with no strings attached! Like all other super contributions, you can't access the co-contribution payment until you reach your preservation age and retire, and you can't split this with your spouse.

You don't have to fill in an application form or do anything else to receive a co-contribution payment (apart from make your non-concessional contribution). But you need to lodge a tax return disclosing the taxable income you derived during the financial year. Your tax return will be checked to see whether you're eligible to receive the payment (see At a glance: super co-contribution eligibility test overleaf). If you satisfy all the conditions, your super fund will notify you when the super co-contribution payment is received from the Tax Office and credited to your account in the following financial year. The co-contribution will also be recorded on your annual member benefit statement (see chapter 1). The Tax Office will also notify you. For more information see the Tax Office publication *Super co-contributions* or you can contact your super fund or refer to your fund's website.

At a glance: super co-contribution eligibility test

You must satisfy the following conditions to qualify for a government co-contribution payment:

- lodge an income tax return

- supply your TFN to your super fund or RSA

- earn less than $61 920

- make a personal after-tax non-concessional contribution to a complying super fund or RSA

- be an Australian resident (for instance, you do not hold a temporary visa at any time during the financial year)

- be less than 71 years of age at the end of the financial year in which the eligible contribution is made

- satisfy an income test and a 10 per cent eligible income test: this means that you must earn at least 10 per cent of your total income from eligible employment-related activities (for instance, receive salary and wages and allowances), carrying on a business or a combination of both.

Self-employed individuals are also eligible for a super co-contribution payment.

Tax tip

According to the Tax Office *total income* is calculated by adding your income attributable to eligible employment-related activities, business and other income to your reportable fringe benefits and reportable employer superannuation contributions, and then subtracting your allowable business deductions.

Case study: superannuation co-contribution scheme

Margaret is a 55-year-old part-time fashion designer earning a salary of $27 000. This is her sole source of income. Under the super guarantee legislation her employer must contribute $2430 to her nominated complying super fund. To help boost her super balance, during the financial year Margaret made a $1000 personal after-tax non-concessional contribution to her super fund. As Margaret's total income is less than $31 920 (and she satisfies all the eligibility tests), the Tax Office will make a $1000 super co-contribution payment on her behalf to her nominated super fund. But she needs to lodge a tax return before she becomes eligible to receive the payment. If Margaret's total income was $40 000, and she made a $1000 personal after-tax non-concessional contribution to her super fund, the super co-contribution payment reduces from $1000 to $731. This is how the lower super co-contribution payment is calculated:

$$\$1000 - [(0.03333 \times (\$40\,000 - \$31\,920)] = \$731.$$

Spouse contribution tax offset

To help low-income earning spouses or non-working spouses boost their superannuation fund balances, the federal government has introduced spouse contributions, so that an individual can make a superannuation contribution on behalf of their spouse. Under this scheme, if your spouse's total assessable income and reportable fringe benefits is less than $10 800, and you make a maximum $3000 super contribution on behalf of your spouse to a complying super fund or RSA, you could qualify for a maximum $540 superannuation spouse contribution tax offset. If your spouse earns more than $10 800 the amount of the tax offset you can claim reduces by 18 cents for every dollar your spouse earns above $10 800, and ceases once your spouse earns more than $13 800. The tax offset can be used to reduce the tax payable on your taxable income. As with all super contributions, your spouse cannot withdraw the money you contribute until they reach their preservation age and satisfy a condition of release (such as retiring). For more details see the Tax Office publication *Superannuation spouse contribution tax offset*.

At a glance: spouse contribution tax offset eligibility test

You need to satisfy the following conditions to qualify for a superannuation spouse contribution tax offset (maximum allowed $540):

- You are married or in a de facto relationship (same-sex couples also qualify).

- Your spouse's assessable income and reportable fringe benefits must not exceed $13 800.

- You did not claim a tax deduction in respect of the contribution you made on behalf of your spouse.

- You must make a spouse contribution to a complying super fund or RSA (maximum permitted $3000).

- You and your spouse are Australian residents at the time you make the contribution and live together on a permanent basis.

- If your spouse is over 65 years of age and less than 70 years of age, your spouse must have satisfied the work test; in other words, worked at least 40 hours in 30 consecutive days in the financial year in which the contribution is made.

Case study: spouse contribution

Henry is married to Louisa who is 56 years of age. His spouse's assessable income and reportable fringe benefits is $13000. During the financial year, Henry made a $3000 superannuation contribution on behalf of his spouse to a complying superannuation fund. As Henry satisfies all the eligibility tests, he can claim a $144 tax offset against the tax payable on the taxable income he derived. This is how the tax offset is calculated:

$$\$540 - [(\$13\,000 - \$10\,800) \times 18 \text{ cents}] = \$144.$$

Self-employed contributions

A self-employed person is a person who receives no superannuation support (for instance, is a sole trader carrying on a small business). There are strict tests to check whether you're genuinely self-employed or an employee (see Employee or contractor? on p. 107). This is an important test, because if you're self-employed and you make a personal pre-tax concessional contribution, the amount you contribute is a tax-deductible expense. A self-employed person can claim a tax deduction up to age 75 years.

The maximum concessional contribution you can make each financial year is limited to $25000 if you're under 50 years of age, and $50000 if you're over 50 years of age. The federal Labor government has proposed that from 1 July 2012, the maximum for those over age 50 will reduce from $50 000 to $25 000. But the good news is you can still make a maximum $50 000 concessional contribution if you're over 50 years of age and your superannuation fund account balance is less than $500 000 (see figure 5.1 on p. 85).

Substantially self-employed

A substantially self-employed person is a person who derives less than 10 per cent of their assessable income from a superannuation-supported source. This is commonly known as the maximum earnings test (see Tax Office Ruling TR 2009/D3: *Income tax: superannuation contributions*). For instance, this could arise if your income comes mainly from investments or you're self-employed, and you derive less than 10 per cent of your assessable income from salary and wages; see appendix B, Substantially self-employed (10 per cent rule). If you satisfy the 10 per cent rule test and make a personal pre-tax concessional contribution, the amount you contribute will qualify as a tax-deductible expense. But, as is the case if you're self-employed, the maximum concessional contributions you can make each financial year are limited to $25 000 if you're under 50 years of age, and $50 000 if you're over 50 years of age.

Tax tip

An SMSF can accept certain in-specie (or non-cash) contributions from its members. The three types of assets you can transfer to your super fund at market value are:

⇒ Business real property, which is your business premises that you use wholly and exclusively to run your business activities, such as your factory, warehouse or office premises (see chapter 4).

⇒ Listed securities, such as shares listed on the Australian Securities Exchange (see chapter 4).

⇒ In-house investment assets, provided they do not exceed 5 per cent of the market value of your super fund's total asset holdings (see chapter 4).

Case study: substantially self-employed

Gerry is 45 years of age and carries on a small plumbing business. During the financial year he made a $20000 personal pre-tax concessional contribution to his SMSF. At the end of the financial year his accounting records showed he derived $100000 from his plumbing activities. During the financial year Gerry taught plumbing at the local trade school. His employer paid him a $5000 salary and made a $450 employer super guarantee contribution to his nominated fund. As Gerry derived less than 10 per cent of his total assessable income ($105 000) from a superannuation-supported source ($5000), he is considered to be substantially self-employed. The $20 000 concessional contribution he made to his super fund is therefore a tax-deductible expense.

If, however, Gerry had derived a $20 000 salary from his teaching activities, he would have failed the substantially self-employed test. This is because more than 10 per cent of his total assessable income ($120 000) came from a superannuation supported source ($20 000). Under these circumstances, Gerry would be ineligible to claim a tax deduction in respect of the $20 000 personal superannuation contribution he made to his SMSF. Under these circumstances, the contributions would be treated as non-concessional contributions, rather than concessional contributions.

Employee or contractor?

As employers have a statutory obligation to make super contributions to a complying super fund on behalf of their employees, you need to establish at the outset whether you are an employee or contractor. The Tax Office defines employees as persons engaged to perform services for salaries and wages; persons working under a contract wholly or principally for their labour; paid company directors; and certain sports persons, artists and performers. For more details see Tax Office Ruling TR 2010/1: *Income tax: superannuation contributions.*

Two major advantages of being classified as a contractor are that your payments are not liable to pay-as-you-go (PAYG) withholding tax, and you can claim certain tax deductions that are not ordinarily available to employees (such as car expenses and superannuation contributions to your complying super fund).

There is often a fine line as to whether you should be classified as an employee or contractor. The following tests are ordinarily used to determine your employment status:

- *Results test.* This test checks whether you are paid to produce a specific result or task; whether you are required to supply your own tools and equipment; and whether you are responsible for your own work and for fixing defects.

- *Control test.* This test checks whether you can delegate tasks to other people if you're unable to complete the task; to what extent you have control as to how the task should be completed; when you can do it; and how you should be paid.

As a general rule you're considered to be a contractor if you satisfy the following key tests:

- You normally advertise for jobs.

- You normally work at different locations.

- You supply your own tools and equipment to complete each task.

- You are required to fix errors and defects.

- You can delegate work to other people to complete each task.

- You have control as to how each task should be completed.

- You can set your own hours to complete each task.

- You prepare a tax invoice setting out services rendered on completion of each task you perform, and charge GST if you're registered or required to be registered.

If you're not sure of your employment status, it's best to consult a professional accountant or registered tax agent. You can also read the Tax Office publication *PAYG withholding guide no 2—how to determine if workers are employees or independent contractors*. You can download a copy from the Tax Office website at <www.ato.gov.au>. See also appendix B, Employees and independent contractors, and Superannuation guarantee charge.

 Tax trap

The Tax Office has prepared an *Employee/contractor decision tool* to help you check whether you are an employee. The Tax Office has also issued Superannuation Guarantee Ruling SGR 2005/1: *Superannuation guarantee: who is an employee?*

Tax trap

If you're classified as a contractor you need to apply for an Australian business number (ABN), and register for GST if your annual turnover (sales) exceeds $75000. You may also need to prepare a business activity statement (BAS) and pay tax on a quarterly basis.

Rollovers from other complying superannuation funds

If you're dissatisfied with your super fund's performance or would like to amalgamate a number of small super funds that you currently belong to, you can roll over (transfer) your benefits from one complying super fund to another complying super fund. You can also roll over your benefits to your SMSF (see chapter 3). You need to complete *Rollover benefit statement* (NAT 70945) and provide documentary evidence (such as certified copies of your driver licence or passport) to prove that these benefits belong to you. You can get a copy of the statement from the Tax Office website or contact your superannuation fund(s).

At the time of transfer, your existing super fund may charge you an administration fee or an exit fee or both. The trustee must roll over your benefits within 30 days of receiving your request. On the other side of the fence, your new super fund may charge you a deposit fee, and you will need to take out a new death and disability insurance policy if you want this insurance cover through your fund. If you roll over your benefits to another complying superannuation fund, no 15 per cent contributions tax is payable because the rollover contributions are coming from a previously taxed source. For more details see the Tax Office publication *How to complete a rollover benefits statement* (NAT 70945).

Tax tip

A free federal government service called Super Fund Lookup provides general information about super funds that have an ABN. For instance, you can check whether the fund is a complying super fund and whether the fund (and more particularly an SMSF) can accept rollovers and super fund contributions. Super funds can also help you to track down lost super (see chapter 1).

Tax trap

If you roll over your benefits the trustee will transfer a cash amount to your new fund. So you may incur CGT on the sale of certain investment assets held in your old super fund. This will be deducted from your benefits before they are transferred. Your new fund will notify you of the actual amount that was rolled over and the date it was credited to your new account.

Partnerships and superannuation

If you carry on a business in partnership, a partner of a partnership can claim a tax deduction for concessional contributions made on behalf of the employees of the partnership. But a partnership cannot claim a tax deduction in respect of any superannuation contributions the partnership makes on behalf of the partners. This is because, under Australian tax law, a partner is not an employee of the partnership. Nevertheless, a partner may qualify for a tax deduction for personal superannuation contributions they make in their individual income tax return. This is on the condition that they are self-employed or substantially self-employed (they satisfy the 10 per cent rule test). For more information see the Tax Office publication *Personal superannuation contributions*.

Useful references

- Australian Securities & Investments Commission consumer website <www.moneysmart.gov.au>. Go to 'About financial products', choose 'Superannuation' and click on 'Building your super'.

Australian Taxation Office publications

- *Contributions splitting application* (NAT 15237)

- *Deduction for personal super contributions: how to complete your notice of intent to claim or vary a deduction for personal super contributions* (NAT 71121)

- *Excess contributions tax—applying to have your contributions disregarded or reallocated*
- *Salary sacrificing super—information for employers*
- Super guarantee (SG) contributions calculator on the ATO website <www.ato.gov.au>
- *Tips to help you keep track of your super contributions*

Australian Taxation Office interpretative decisions

- ID 2010/217: *CGT small business concessions: retirement exemption— contribution to complying superannuation fund—transfer of real property*

Other taxation rulings

- SGR 2005/1: *Superannuation guarantee: who is an employee?*
- TA 2010/2: *Circumvention of excess contributions tax*
- TA 2010/3: *Non market value acquisition of shares or share options by a self-managed superannuation fund*

Chapter 6

Sharing your wealth: taxing your accumulated benefits

There are two distinct phases or periods in the life cycle of a complying super fund. They are referred to as the accumulation phase, when member contributions are invested on their behalf, and the pension phase, when members can access their benefits once they satisfy a condition of release. Different tax rules apply to each phase of the super fund's life cycle. In this chapter I discuss the tax issues relating to super fund members and how complying superannuation funds are taxed.

How the Australian tax system works

After the end of the financial year, which commences on 1 July and ends on 30 June each year, a superannuation fund must lodge a superannuation fund tax return by 31 October, disclosing the taxable income they earned during the financial year. Taxable income is defined as assessable income less allowable deductions. The *Income Tax Assessment Act 1997* sets out the rules for determining what earnings are assessable and what losses or outgoings are allowable deductions.

At a glance: how complying super funds are taxed

This is how a complying superannuation fund is taxed under Australian tax law:

- Complying super funds pay tax at the rate of 15 per cent on the taxable income they derive, while non-complying super funds pay tax at the rate of 45 per cent.

- Under the CGT provisions, only two-thirds of any capital gains a super fund makes on sale of CGT assets held for more than 12 months is liable to a 15 per cent rate of tax. But the entire amount is taxed at the rate of 15 per cent if CGT assets are bought and sold within 12 months.

- Assessable contributions (such as concessional, or pre-tax, contributions) are included as part of a superannuation fund's total assessable income and are liable to 15 per cent contributions tax.

- Non-concessional (after-tax) contributions are not included as part of a superannuation fund's total assessable income and are not liable to 15 per cent contributions tax.

- All super pensions and cash withdrawals payable to members after they turn 60 years of age and retire are exempt from tax. Members who receive a super pension and are aged between 55 and 59 years pay tax at their marginal rates, but qualify for a 15 per cent tax offset.

- Income and capital gains that a super fund derives during the pension phase to fund pension payments are exempt from tax.

- The trustee of an SMSF must apply for a tax file number and lodge a *Self-managed superannuation fund annual return*, disclosing the super fund's taxable income.

- Dividends paid from a private company to an SMSF are ordinarily treated as special income and are liable to tax at the rate of 45 per cent (rather than 15 per cent).

Tax trap

The Tax Office has issued a publication entitled *Industries at high risk of not complying with super-annuation.* These industries are accommodation (housekeepers, receptionists and hotel staff), accounting (accountants and accounting clerks), computer system design and related services (software and applications) and programmers and ICT (information and communication technology) managers. This means the Tax Office is watching these industries to ensure the correct amount of superannuation payments are being made on behalf of their employees.

Contributions and taxation

The government has created a number of tax incentives to encourage you to make a contribution to a complying superannuation fund. The fund invests these contributions on your behalf and they cannot be accessed until you satisfy a condition of release, such as when you retire (see chapter 8). The tax issues you need to consider depends on whether the contribution you or your employer are making is classified as a concessional contribution or non-concessional contribution. Further, the federal government has introduced a number of tax incentives to help low-income earners boost their retirement benefits (see chapter 5).

Concessional contributions

Concessional contributions (or pre-tax contributions) are contributions you make to a complying super fund that qualify for a tax deduction. Under Australian tax law, a deduction is allowed in the financial year in which you make the contribution. As these contributions are tax deductible, your super fund treats them as assessable contributions and so 15 per cent contributions tax is deducted from these contributions. For instance, if you make a $10000 concessional contribution, your super fund has to pay $1500 tax on this amount. Only employers, the self-employed and individuals who are substantially self-employed can make concessional contributions and claim a tax deduction. Employees cannot make concessional contributions, nor can they claim a tax deduction for the amount they contribute (see chapter 5).

 Tax tip

If you make a concessional contribution, you need to forward to your super fund a *Notice of intent to claim a tax deduction for super contributions or vary a previous notice* (NAT 71121), and specify the amount you intend to claim. The trustee must acknowledge your notification and the amount you're claiming, before you lodge your personal income tax return. You need to do this in order for your super fund to treat the contribution as an assessable contribution. For more details see the Tax Office publication *Deduction for personal super contributions* (NAT 71121).

Tax tip

Interest incurred on borrowings to finance concessional contributions to a complying super fund that qualify for a tax deduction is a tax-deductible expense. But this is not the case if you borrow money to finance non-concessional contributions that don't qualify for a tax deduction.

Concessional contribution cap amount

A concessional contribution cap amount limits the amount of concessional contributions you can make to a complying super fund each financial year. The concessional contribution cap amount depends on your age at the time you make the contribution.

For the financial year ended 30 June 2012, the concessional contribution cap amount is $25 000 if you're less than 50 years of age, and $50 000 if you're over 50 years of age (see figure 5.1 on p. 85). The $25 000 cap is indexed annually and is rounded down to the nearest multiple of $5000. From 1 July 2012 if you're over 50 years of age the concessional contribution cap will reduce from $50 000 to $25 000. But the good news here is the federal Labor government has proposed that the cap will remain at $50 000 if your super fund balance is below $500 000. If you breach this cap, you're liable to pay excess concessional contributions tax (see figure 5.1 on p. 85).

Excess concessional contributions tax

If you exceed the concessional contribution cap the excess amount is taxed at the rate of 31.5 per cent. This effectively means you will be liable to pay 46.5 per cent tax on the excess (namely 15 per cent contributions tax + 31.5 per cent excess concessional contributions tax). The additional tax is referred to as excess concessional contributions tax. Any excess concessional contributions can count as non-concessional contributions. Your super fund must report this contravention to the Tax Office. If you're notified that you're liable to pay the excess concessional contributions tax you can pay the tax yourself. Alternatively, you can prepare a voluntary release authority and ask your super fund to release funds to help you meet your obligation to pay the tax. You can also use a combination of both payment methods. You must pay this tax within 21 days of receiving the notification. For more details see the Tax Office publication *Super contributions—too much super can mean extra tax.*

 Tax trap

Concessional contributions are tax deductible to the extent that you have a taxable income. This is because under Australian tax law concessional contributions can't be taken into account to create or increase a tax loss. For instance, if your taxable income is $25 000, and you make a $35 000 concessional contribution that qualifies for a tax

> **Tax trap** *(cont'd)*
>
> deduction, your tax deduction is limited to $25 000, as the $10 000 excess will create a tax loss that cannot be claimed. Further, keep in kind that once your taxable income falls below $16 000 no tax is payable on this amount as you can claim a low-income tax offset; see appendix A, table 3.

Non-concessional contributions

Non-concessional contributions (or after-tax contributions) are personal contributions you make to a complying superannuation fund that don't qualify for a tax deduction. Anyone who is under 65 years of age can make a non-concessional contribution. Because these contributions are treated as capital contributions, your super fund does not have to pay 15 per cent contributions tax on the contribution, as is the case if you make a concessional contribution. To add icing to the contribution cake, these contributions are not liable to tax at the time they are withdrawn from your super fund (see chapter 8).

Non-concessional contribution cap

A non-concessional contribution cap amount limits the amount you can contribute to your super fund each year. For the financial year ended 30 June 2012 the non-concessional contribution cap amount is $150000 if you're under 65 years of age. Further, if you're less than 65 years of age, you can make non-concessional contributions up to a maximum of $450000 during the financial year. But if you do this, you can't make any further non-concessional contributions for the next two financial years. Once you turn 65 years of age you need to satisfy the work test if you want to make a non-concessional contribution, and the maximum you can contribute each year is limited to $150000. To comply with the work test you need to work a minimum of 40 hours over a consecutive 30-day period during financial year. Once you turn 75 years of age you can no longer make non-concessional contributions. If you exceed the non-concessional contribution cap, the excess amount is taxed at the rate of 46.5 per cent (see figure 5.1 on p. 85).

The accumulation phase

During the super fund's accumulation phase, where member benefits are accruing on their behalf, the superannuation fund will ordinarily derive its assessable income from three major sources:

- assessable contributions from members that qualify for a tax deduction

- investment income from the fund's investment activities (such as interest, dividends and rent)

- capital gains on sale of CGT assets (such as shares and property).

Assessable contributions

If you intend to claim a tax deduction for concessional contributions you make to a complying super fund, you need to lodge a *Notice of intent to claim a tax deduction for super contributions or vary a previous notice* (NAT 71121) and specify the amount you intend to claim. When you do this, your super fund will notify you that your intention to claim a tax deduction has been acknowledged. The letter of acknowledgement must be included when you lodge your individual tax return. The amount you contribute is treated as part of your super fund's assessable income and is liable to a 15 per cent contributions tax, which is deducted from your account.

Case study: claiming a tax deduction

During the financial year the XYZ complying superannuation fund received a $20000 personal pre-tax concessional contribution from a self-employed member. The member, who is aged less than 50 years, had lodged a notification of intent to claim a $20000 tax deduction for the financial year ended 20XX. Under these circumstances, the fund will treat the $20000 concessional contribution as assessable contributions and liable to a 15 per cent contributions tax. The member can claim a tax deduction when her super fund issues a notification acknowledging the intention to claim a tax deduction and amount that will be claimed.

Investment income

The investment income your super fund derives from its investment activities (such as interest, dividends and rent) is included as part of the super fund's total assessable income and liable to tax at the rate of 15 per cent.

Dividends and franking credits

Under Australian tax law, when a company pays a dividend it must tell its shareholders (for instance, your super fund) whether the dividend is franked or unfranked. If the dividend is franked, your super fund will receive a dividend franking credit (or tax offset) that can be applied against the tax payable. The size of the dividend franking credit depends on whether the company had paid tax on its profits and to what extent the dividend is franked. A dividend payment can be either fully franked (meaning your fund will get a 100 per cent franking credit), partially franked (for instance, your fund will get a 50 per cent franking credit) or unfranked (meaning your fund will get no franking credits). The following formula is used to calculate a fully franked dividend:

$$\text{Cash dividend} \times 30 \div 70 = \text{franking credit}$$

Incidentally, $30 \div 70$ is the company tax rate $(0.30) \div (1 - \text{company tax rate: } 0.70)$ For instance, if your super fund receives a \$1000 fully franked dividend your super fund will receive \$1000 in cash plus a \$428 dividend franking credit ($\$1000 \times 30 \div 70 = \$428$).

You need to include both the franked dividend amount ($1000 in this case) and dividend franking credit ($428 in this case) as part of your super fund's total assessable income. But the great news here is the dividend franking credits ($428 in this case) can be offset against the gross tax payable. If the total dividend franking credits exceed the gross tax payable the excess amount is refunded to your super fund.

Case study: receiving a dividend franking credit

During the financial year an SMSF received a $10000 fully franked dividend from CBA Ltd. The dividend franking credit was $4286 ($10000 × 30/70 = $4286). This was the super fund's sole source of income and the fund's deductible expenses amounted to $500. The super fund needs to include the $10000 franked dividend amount and $4286 dividend franking credit as part of its total assessable income ($10000 + $4286 = $14286), and the fund can claim a $4286 tax offset against the gross tax payable. If the dividend was partially franked (for instance, 50 per cent was franked) the dividend franking credit is reduced by 50 per cent to $2143 ($10000 × 30/70 × 50 per cent = 2143).

Table 6.1 shows how the taxable income is calculated.

Table 6.1: calculation of taxable income for an SMSF receiving franked dividends

Calculation of taxable income	Amount
Taxable income	
Franked dividend amount	$10000

Calculation of taxable income	Amount
Dividend franking credit	$4286
Total income	$14286
Less	
Deductions	$500
Taxable income	$13786

Table 6.2 shows how an SMSF is taxed.

Table 6.2: income tax calculation statement for an SMSF

Tax and supervisory levy		Amount
Gross tax	($13786 × 15%)	$2067
Supervisory levy		$180
Total payable		$2247
Less		
Dividend franking credit		$4286
Tax refund		$2039

Note: An SMSF is liable to pay a $180 supervisory levy at the time it lodges a self managed superannuation fund annual return.

As the total dividend franking credits ($4286) exceed the gross tax payable (plus a $180 supervisory levy) ($2247), the excess amount ($2039) is refunded to the super fund.

Dividend franking credits and the 45-day rule

To qualify for a dividend franking credit your super fund must hold the shares at risk (meaning that your shares could fall in value) for a minimum of 45 days (not including the purchase date and sale date). The holding period increases to 90 days for certain preference shares. If you fail to meet this technical condition, your super fund cannot claim a dividend franking credit. Further, your super fund is ineligible to claim the $5000 small shareholder threshold amount that's available to individual shareholders who receive a total of $5000 or fewer dividend franking credits. For more details see the Tax Office publication *Company tax franking credits: overview* (NAT 5849). You can download a copy from the Tax Office website <www.ato.gov.au>.

Capital gains

If your super fund makes a capital gain on the sale of CGT assets (such as shares, real estate and units in a property trust) during the super fund's accumulation phase, the capital gain is liable to tax. The amount of tax your super fund must pay depends on whether the CGT asset was owned for more than 12 months. This is how the tax is calculated:

- Only two-thirds of the capital gain is taxable at the rate of 15 per cent if the CGT asset was owned by the fund for more than 12 months.

- The entire capital gain is taxable at the rate of 15 per cent if the fund buys and sells a CGT asset within 12 months.

On the other hand, if the fund makes a capital loss on the sale of a CGT asset, the capital loss can be deducted only from a capital gain made in another asset sale. If the super fund makes no capital gains in the year the financial loss is made, the capital loss can be carried forward for an indefinite period until the super fund makes a capital gain.

If a super fund makes a capital gain on sale of CGT assets when the fund is in the pension phase, the entire capital gain is exempt from tax (see The pension phase on p. 137).

 Tax tip

A capital gain arises when the capital proceeds (or sale price) from the sale of a CGT asset is more than the CGT asset's cost base (for instance, the purchase price plus certain costs you have incurred, such as buying and selling costs).

 Tax tip

A capital loss arises when the capital proceeds (or sale price) on sale of a CGT asset is less than the CGT asset's reduced cost base (for instance, the purchase

Case study: making a capital gain

Three years ago the trustee of an SMSF purchased 1000 shares in XYZ Ltd at $10 per share (total cost $10 000) and paid $100 brokerage fee and GST. Today the trustee has sold the 1000 shares in XYZ Ltd and received $15 per share ($15 000) and paid $150 brokerage fee and GST. Table 6.3 shows how the CGT is calculated.

Table 6.3: calculation of CGT on the sale of SMSF assets

CGT formula	Amount
Capital proceeds (sale price)	$15 000
Less	
Cost base	
Purchase price	$10 000
Purchase costs (brokerage fee and GST)	$100
Sale costs (brokerage fee and GST)	$150
Total cost base	$10 250

CGT formula	Amount
Notional capital gain	$4750
Taxable capital gain ($4750 × 2/3)	$3166
Gross tax ($3166 × 15 per cent) payable	$475

As the shares were owned for more than 12 months, only two-thirds of the capital gain is liable to tax (in this case $3166) at the rate of 15 per cent. This means that the entire capital gain ($4750) is effectively taxed at the rate of 10 per cent. (But if the shares were bought and sold within 12 months the entire capital gain would have been taxed at the rate of 15 per cent.)

If the capital proceeds on sale were $5000 the super fund would have made a $5250 capital loss ($10 250 − $5000 = $5250).

Capital gains and small business

If you carry on a small business you could qualify for a number of tax concessions. Under Australian tax law, you're considered to be running a small business if your annual turnover (sales) is less than $2 million per year. If your turnover is higher than this, your net business assets cannot exceed $6 million for your enterprise to be classed as a small business.

One significant tax concession is available under the small business CGT retirement provisions. An individual can claim a $500 000 lifetime retirement exemption on the sale of active business assets, such as plant and equipment and business premises. The capital gain that is exempt is called the CGT exempt amount. If you are a sole trader or in partnership and you are over 55 years of age, capital gains up to your $500 000 lifetime limit are exempt from tax. You can keep the cash from the sale or put it into a complying super fund or retirement savings account (RSA).

If you're less than 55 years of age, for the capital gain to be exempt, you must immediately contribute the CGT exempt amount into a complying super fund or RSA. This means you can't access the funds until you reach your preservation age and satisfy a condition of relief (see chapter 8).

Different rules apply if the business assets are owned by a trust or company. For more information, see the Tax Office publication *Retirement exemption—capital gains tax concession for small business.*

 Tax trap

An SMSF is prohibited from deriving income from carrying on a business (such as a share-trading business). If you carry on a business, there's a risk that your super fund could contravene the sole purpose test (see chapter 4).

Allowable deductions

Under Australian tax law, you can deduct from your assessable income any loss or outgoing (payment) to the extent that it is incurred in gaining or producing your assessable income. Expressed simply, for a loss or outgoing to qualify as a tax-deductible expense, there must be a relevant and necessary connection between the expenditure you incur and the derivation of assessable income. The Tax Office has issued Tax Office Ruling TR 93/17: *Income tax: income tax deductions available to superannuation funds* to explain what types of losses and outgoings a superannuation fund can claim. The common types of tax deductions a superannuation fund, and more particularly an SMSF, can claim are:

- actuarial costs
- accountancy fees
- approved audit fee
- death benefit increase (see chapter 9)
- capital works deduction (rental properties)
- death and disability premiums
- depreciation of assets (rental property)
- insurance premiums (rental property)
- interest expenses
- investment expenses
- legal costs
- management and administration expenses
- tax agent fees.

Self managed super funds tax return

At the end of each financial year the trustee must lodge a *Self-managed superannuation fund annual return* by 31 October disclosing the fund's taxable income. The Tax Office has advised that refusal to lodge a tax return or not lodging a tax return on time are common mistakes with SMSFs. This contravention could cause a complying super fund to become a non-complying fund and lose its tax concessions. When the return is lodged the Tax Office will add a $180 supervisory levy to the gross tax payable (see the following case study).

 Tax trap

The accounts of an SMSF must be audited each year by an approved auditor before lodgment of the *Self-managed superannuation fund annual return*. The auditor must provide the audit report to the trustees and report any contraventions to the Tax Office (see chapter 4).

Case study: calculating the taxable income

During the financial year, an SMSF received a $25 000 personal superannuation contribution from a self-employed member who was less than 50 years of age. The member has informed the trustee that they intend to claim a tax deduction for the contribution they made. Under these circumstances, the $25000 personal contribution will be treated as an assessable contribution. During the financial year, the super fund also received $35000 fully franked dividends from its investment activities, and the dividend franking credits were $15000. The super fund also made a $24000 capital gain on sale of shares that were owned for more than 12 months. The super fund's management and administration expenses were $4000. Table 6.4 shows the SMSF's taxable income and deductions.

Table 6.4: calculation of an SMSF's income and deductions

Calculating the taxable income	Amount
Income	
Assessable contributions	$25000
Dividends	
Franked amount	$35000
Franking credit	$15000
Net capital gain	$16000
Total assessable income	**$91000**
Less	
Deductions	
Management and administration expenses	$4000
Taxable income	**$87000**

Table 6.5 shows how income tax is calculated for the SMSF, based on the amounts shown in table 6.4.

Table 6.5: calculation of income tax for the SMSF

Tax and supervisory levy	Amount
Taxable income	$87 000
Gross tax ($87 000 × 15 per cent)	$13 050
Supervisory levy	$180
Total payable	$13 230
Less	
Dividend franking credits	$15 000
Total amount refundable	$1770

Here's an explanation of some of the entries in tables 6.4 and 6.5.

⇒ As the shares were owned for more than 12 months, only two-thirds of the capital gain is liable to tax ($24 000 × 2/3 = $16 000).

⇒ At the time of lodgement, the SMSF must pay a $180 supervisory levy.

⇒ The SMSF must receive an audit report from an approved auditor before it can lodge its *Self-managed superannuation fund annual return*.

The pension phase

When a complying super fund (and more particularly an SMSF) is in the pension phase, all investment income earned and all capital gains on the sale of CGT assets to fund pension payments are exempt from tax. In addition, all dividend franking credits are refunded to your super fund (see Dividends and franking credits on p. 125). For a super fund to be in the pension phase, the relevant member must satisfy a condition of release. The most common way to meet this condition is reaching preservation age and retiring from the workforce (see chapter 8). (If there are other members who have not yet retired, their respective benefits will still be in the accumulation phase.)

 Tax tip

If you don't need to lodge an SMSF tax return (for instance, your super fund has terminated), you need to complete a *Lodgment of income tax return/s not necessary* (NAT TX 160) form with the Tax Office.

Useful references
Australian Taxation Office publications

- *Refunding excess imputation credits—superannuation funds, approved deposit funds and pooled super-annuation trusts*

- *Super and capital gains tax*

- *Super co-contributions*
- *Super contributions — too much super can mean extra tax*

Australian Taxation Office interpretative decisions

- ID 2002/371: *Superannuation Part IX taxation of superannuation entities — superannuation fund expenses — trauma policy*
- ID 2010/76: *Superannuation benefits: deduction for insurance — increase in the untaxed element*

Chapter 7

Building wealth: accumulating retirement benefits

The sole purpose of building wealth in a complying super fund must be to provide retirement benefits to members, and benefits to dependants in the event of a member's death. A significant advantage of running an SMSF is your capacity to choose your own investments to fulfil these core conditions. Although this may seem like a great idea, you need to weigh up your personal commitment, the rules you must comply with, and whether you can consistently outperform the professionally managed super funds. In this chapter, I explain the different types of asset classes an SMSF can own to help fund retirement strategies, and the key principles of investing.

Investment strategy

The trustees of an SMSF are permitted to purchase certain approved asset classes to help maximise member benefits and fund retirement strategies. To do this by the book, the trustees must prepare and implement an investment strategy. All investment decisions must be made in accordance with the fund's investment strategy, and they must not contravene the SIS Act. If in doubt the trustees should seek professional advice. And any advice they receive should be documented. According to the SIS Act, having an investment strategy provides a defence for trustees against an action by a member for loss or damages suffered as a result of the trustee making an investment. This is on the condition that the trustees have acted in good faith in accordance with the fund's investment strategy. The investment strategy must be in writing and should consider the following important issues:

- *The fund's objectives.* The trustees must set out your core objectives (for instance, to achieve a certain rate of return), and the steps you intend to take to achieve those objectives.

- *Diversification.* The trustees must list the different types of asset classes you plan to hold to achieve your objectives (such as shares, fixed interest securities, real estate, managed funds and collectables).

- *Investment risk.* The trustees must consider the risks involved for each of the different asset classes you plan to hold. This is extremely important as certain investment assets (particularly shares) can decrease in value, which could have an adverse effect on member benefits.

- *Investment yield.* The trustees must note the return you believe you are likely to receive on your investment portfolio.

- *Liquidity.* The trustees must set out your fund's ability to pay retirement benefits (pensions) and the various ongoing costs you're likely to incur when pensions or lump sums become due and payable. This could become a problem if your super fund owns predominantly investment assets (for instance, property and collectables) that can't be readily sold at short notice.

The trustees must review the investment strategy at regular intervals and make any necessary changes in the best interest of all members. The trustees must also keep proper records to verify the existence of these investment assets (such as a holding statement for shares and a certificate of title for property) and how they're valued. These documents must be produced when your superannuation fund is audited by an independent auditor at the end of each financial year (see chapter 4).

Tax tip

Trustees must keep the assets of the SMSF separate from any personal trustee assets. Further, the trustees of an SMSF should not share a bank account with any other legal entity.

At a glance: eligible investment assets

Eligible asset classes an SMSF can hold include:

- business real property from a related party. Your super fund can purchase your business premises and lease them back to you (see chapter 4)

- certain approved collectables and personal use assets (such as artwork, antiques, rare coins and stamps). However, members cannot gain a personal benefit from them (for instance, display the collectables at a member's home or use and enjoy them). The federal Labor government has proposed that, from 1 July 2011, collectables must be insured and kept in storage, and the trustee must get annual valuations

- derivatives such as call and put options, and contracts for differences. For more details about these investments see the Australian Security Exchange website <www.asx.com.au> and go to 'Self managed super funds', then 'Using ASX listed products in SMSFs'

- fixed interest securities (such as government bonds and term deposits)

- in-house assets (for instance, lease agreements) that do not exceed more than 5 per cent of the market value of the super fund's total investment assets (see chapter 4)

- instalment warrants to buy certain approved investment assets (see chapter 4)

- managed funds operated by major financial institutions

- real estate (such as commercial, industrial and residential property)

- shares listed on the Australian Securities Exchange (ASX).

 Tax tip

An SMSF can acquire investment assets from related parties, including:

⇒ listed securities (for example, shares, units, bonds, debentures, options, interests in managed investment schemes or other securities listed on the ASX)

⇒ business real property at its market value

⇒ certain in-house assets at their market value.

Tax tip *(cont'd)*

For more details see the Tax Office Ruling SMSFR 2010/1: *Self managed superannuation funds: the application of subsection 66(1) of the* Superannuation Industry (Supervision) Act 1993 *to the acquisition of an asset by a self managed superannuation fund from a related party.*

 Tax tip

Trustees should use the market value when reporting the valuation of investment assets held in an SMSF. The SIS Act defines market value as:

the amount that a willing buyer of the asset could reasonably be expected to pay to acquire the asset from a willing seller if the following assumptions were made:

(a) that the buyer and the seller dealt with each other at arm's length in relation to the sale;

(b) that the sale occurred after proper marketing of the asset;

(c) that the buyer and the seller acted knowledgeably and prudentially in relation to the sale.

For more information see the Tax Office Superannuation Circular 2003/1: *Self-managed superannuation funds.*

At a glance: what your SMSF can't do

Your SMSF can't do the following:

- acquire property from a related party (for instance, a main residence from a member or a member's relative)

- lease a residential property your super fund owns to a related party

- lend money to your super fund

- lend money to members or their relatives (for instance, spouse, child or parent).

 Tax trap

The Tax Office has advised a common mistake by SMSFs is making unauthorised loans to the fund's members and their relatives, and receiving loans from members; see appendix B, Loans and self managed super funds.

 Tax trap

An SMSF is not permitted to carry on a business (such as share trading), as the SMSF would then be considered to have contravened the sole purpose test (see chapter 4).

General investment principles

There are many factors you need to compare and consider when putting together a suitable investment portfolio to help maximise member benefits. This is because each asset class will have certain features that may or may not interest you as a trustee. You need to weigh up key factors, such as the income the asset may earn; whether you can expect capital growth; what the tax benefits may be; as well as the volatility, liquidity, entry and exit fees and holding costs (see table 7.1) of each asset. An ideal investment is one that has the capacity to deliver long-term capital growth while also paying you a regular income stream. The most common investments your super fund is likely to consider are:

- shares

- fixed interest securities

- real estate

- managed funds

- collectables.

Table 7.1: investment asset classes at a glance

Benefits	Shares	Fixed interest securities	Real estate	Managed funds	Collectables
Income	Yes	Yes	Yes	Yes	No
Capital growth	Yes	No	Yes	Yes	Yes

Benefits	Shares	Fixed interest securities	Real estate	Managed funds	Collectables
Tax benefits	Yes	No	Yes	Yes	Yes
Volatility	High	Minimal	Medium	Medium	Low
Liquidity	High	High	Low	High	Low
Entry fee	Minimal	No	High	Minimal	High
Exit fee	Minimal	No	High	Minimal	High
Holding costs	No	No	Yes	Yes	Yes

 Tax tip

The Tax Office publishes regular statistical information of the different types of assets held by SMSFs. You can find this information on the ATO website: search for 'Self-managed super fund statistical report'.

Shares

When you invest in the share market you will be buying shares in major Australian companies that are listed on the ASX, such as BHP Billiton, the Commonwealth Bank (CBA) and Woolworths. You will be relying on these companies running profitable businesses to provide you with a steady income stream in the form of dividends, and long-term capital growth. You will generally find capital growth depends primarily on a company's capacity to continually expand its business operations and boost profits. The more profitable these companies become, the more likely it is that your fund's investment portfolio will appreciate in value. So it's important that you understand what these companies do to generate sales and whether they're trading profitably. A stockbroker can help you with this exercise.

When you invest in shares listed on the ASX, you need to be aware of four major documents. These documents are:

- *Buy contract note.* When you buy shares your stockbroker will issue a buy contract note setting out details such as the purchase price, the number of shares you bought, and your purchase costs. You need this information to calculate the cost base of your shares (see chapter 6).

- *Holding statement.* Shortly after you buy your shares, the company you have invested in will send you a holding statement setting out the number of shares you own in the company. This document proves that you are the owner of these shares.

- *Sell contract note.* When you sell shares your stockbroker will issue a sell contract note setting out details such as the sale price, the number of shares you sold, and your sale costs. The buy and sell contract notes can be used to quickly calculate the amount of capital gain or capital loss you made on the sale (see chapter 6).

- *Dividend statements.* Once you have bought shares you become a part-owner of the company, and so you're eligible to receive a share of the company's profits, which are referred to as dividends. When a company pays you a dividend, it will issue a dividend statement setting out the amount of dividends you were paid, and the dividend franking credits you can claim (see chapter 6).

You need to produce all of these documents when your super fund is audited by the approved auditor that you must appoint each year. This is to verify the number of shares your super fund owns, and the amount of dividends and dividend franking credits your fund received. As share prices are published daily you can quickly calculate the market value of all the shares your super fund owns, and check whether they have increased or decreased in value.

At a glance: benefits of investing in shares

The benefits your super fund can gain from investing in the share market are listed here:

- *Income (dividends).* Companies normally declare and pay two dividends each year. They are described as an interim dividend and a final dividend. The average dividend yield of the major companies listed on the ASX is normally around 4 per cent per year, and the grossed-up dividend yield (dividend + franking credit) is normally around 5.2 per cent per year.

- *Capital growth.* A significant benefit from owning shares is their capacity to increase in value. Under Australian tax law, unrealised capital gains are not liable to tax until the shares are sold. To add icing to the capital growth cake, if you sell the shares during the super fund's pension phase, any capital gain you make on sale is free of tax (see chapters 6 and 8).

- *Tax benefits.* These come in two main forms:

  - *Dividend franking credits.* If a company pays your super fund a franked dividend you will receive a dividend franking credit tax offset that you can deduct from the gross tax payable. And if the total dividend franking credits exceed the gross tax payable, the excess amount is refunded to your super fund (see chapter 6).

  - *CGT discount.* If your super fund makes a capital gain on sale of shares during the accumulation phase, only two-thirds of the capital gain is assessable, providing the shares were owned for more than 12 months (see chapter 6).

- *Liquidity.* As shares listed on the ASX can be sold within a matter of seconds; you can quickly access cash at short notice (normally within four days), which means that shares are highly liquid. This is good to know if you need to pay a substantial retirement benefit to a member or lump sum death benefit to a dependant in the event of a member's death (see chapters 8 and 9).

- *Prices published daily.* You can quickly determine the market value of your super fund's share portfolio, and calculate the amount of benefits that members are accumulating in their respective accounts whenever you need to.

- *Entry and exit fees.* The brokerage fees associated with buying and selling shares are minimal (usually around 0.05 per cent of the cost of the shares if bought and sold online). No GST is payable on share transactions, although your super fund will have to pay GST on brokerage fees.

- *No holding costs.* The good news is there are no ongoing holding costs associated with owning shares, as is the case if you invest in real estate, managed funds and collectables.

 Tax trap

To qualify for a dividend franking credit your super fund must hold the shares at risk (meaning that they can fall in value) for at least 45 days (not including the days you buy and sell them). If you fail to meet this condition your super fund cannot claim a dividend franking credit. Further, your super fund is ineligible to claim the $5000 small shareholder threshold amount that's available to individual shareholders.

At a glance: limitations of investing in shares

The limitations of investing in the share market are:

- *Volatility.* As share prices fluctuate daily, there's a major risk that your share portfolio could fall in value, adversely affecting member benefits. Under Australian tax law, an unrealised capital loss cannot be claimed until you sell the shares.

- *Dividend payments could fall.* There's a risk that a company may not pay you a dividend or that the dividend payment could decrease. This could become a major concern if your super fund is in the pension phase, and you're relying on dividends to pay pensions to members.

 Tax trap

If your super fund owns shares in a private company and the trustee receives a dividend from that company, the Tax Office will ordinarily treat the payment as 'special income' and liable to a 45 per cent rate of tax (rather than at the concessional rate of 15 per cent). However, this will not be the case if the Tax Office treats the dividend for tax purposes as 'non-arms length income'. For more information see Tax Office Ruling TR 2006/7: *Income tax: special income derived by*

a complying superannuation fund, a complying approved deposit fund or a pooled superannuation trust in relation to the year of income. See also appendix B, Special income.

Shares: diversification

Trustees of an SMSF are required to consider diversification when preparing an investment strategy, so it's best to invest in a number of companies from different sectors of the Australian economy. A manageable portfolio of around 10 companies may be worth examining. If you do this you won't be putting all your eggs in one basket, and you will avoid any potential disasters that could adversely affect your portfolio if one of these companies were to perform poorly. Further, the more companies you have, the greater the chance of getting into something that could make you a lot of money. A good starting point when putting together a quality share portfolio is to examine the S&P/ASX 20 index (see table 7.2, overleaf). This index consists of the top 20 Australian companies listed on the ASX: it represents more than 50 per cent of the entire wealth of the Australian economy. A financial planner or stockbroker can put together a quality share portfolio to help you maximise member benefits.

Table 7.2: S&P/ASX 20 Index

ASX code	Company name	Sector
AMP	AMP Ltd	Insurance
ANZ	ANZ Banking Group Ltd	Banks
BHP	BHP Billiton Ltd	Materials
BXB	Brambles Ltd	Commercial services and supplies
CBA	Commonwealth Bank of Australia Ltd	Banks
CSL	CSL Ltd	Pharmaceuticals and biotechnology
FGL	Fosters Group Ltd	Food, beverage and tobacco
MQG	Macquarie Group Ltd	Banks
NAB	National Australia Bank Ltd	Banks
NCM	Newcrest Mining Ltd	Materials
ORG	Origin Energy Ltd	Energy
QBE	QBE Insurance Group Ltd	Insurance
RIO	Rio Tinto Ltd	Materials
SUN	Suncorp-Metway Ltd	Banks
TLS	Telstra Corporation Ltd	Telecommunications services

ASX code	Company name	Sector
WBC	Westpac Banking Corporation	Banks
WDC	Westfield Group	Real estate
WES	Wesfarmers Ltd	Food and staples retailing
WOW	Woolworths Ltd	Food and staples retailing
WPL	Woodside Petroleum Ltd	Energy

Source: CommSec

Fixed interest securities

When you invest in fixed interest securities (such as bank bills, term deposits, debentures and government bonds), you will be depositing your money with reputable financial institutions or government authorities that are properly regulated. In return for the use of your money, you will ordinarily receive a fixed rate of interest at regular intervals (for instance, every six months), which you can usually take in cash or have added to the principal. When the loan matures, you will get back the amount you initially invested (plus the interest if you have not taken it in cash). Investing in fixed interest securities may interest you if you feel uncomfortable with alternative assets (such as shares, real estate and managed funds) that can fall in value and adversely affect member benefits.

As superannuation is a long-term retirement strategy you could consider the benefit of compound interest, where you can reinvest the interest you derive and earn interest on your interest. For instance, if you deposit $10 000 in a term deposit for five years, and the interest rate is 7 per cent compounding annually, when the loan matures your initial $10 000 deposit will have increased to $14 025. And the growth rate will be even higher if the interest is paid more frequently (for instance, every three or six months). Under Australian tax law the interest that's allowed to compound in your account each financial year must be included as part of your super fund's taxable income (as is the case if it is paid to you each year), and it is liable to tax at the rate of 15 per cent. For more details see Tax Office interpretative decision ID 2002/886: *Income tax: assessability of compound interest.*

At a glance: benefits of investing in fixed interest securities

The benefits your super fund can gain from investing in fixed interest securities are:

- *Income (interest).* Interest is ordinarily credited to your super fund's account on a monthly, quarterly, half-yearly or yearly basis. Interest rates vary in line with the prevailing market and the term of the investment (currently around 6 per cent).

- *Liquidity.* When the loan matures you will get back the amount you initially invested. This is a worthwhile benefit to have up your sleeve if you need a specific amount of cash to meet a future commitment. This may not be the case if you invest in market-linked securities (such as shares, real estate and managed funds), which can decrease in value.

- *Entry and exit fees.* There are no entry and exit fees, but you could incur a penalty (for instance, receive a lesser amount of interest) if you terminate the investment before the maturity date.

- *No holding costs.* There are no ongoing costs with this class of investment.

At a glance: limitations of investing in fixed interest securities

The limitations, or risks, of investing in fixed interest securities are:

- *No capital growth.* A major drawback with this class of investment is that they don't increase in value (in contrast to shares or real estate, for instance), which could adversely affect member benefits in the long-term.

- *No tax benefits.* There are no tax benefits that you can take advantage of, as is the case if you receive a franked dividend from a share investment.

- *Interest rates could fall.* There's a risk that interest rates could fall, which means the return on your investment will decrease. For instance, you are currently receiving 7 per cent interest on a term deposit. If the best rate you can get when the term deposit matures is 5 per cent, the return on your investment will decrease by 2 per cent if you decide to reinvest your money in another term deposit.

 Tax trap

The federal Labor government has proposed allowing individual investors a 50 per cent discount on the first $1000 of interest on deposits with certain approved financial institutions and on bonds, debentures and annuity products. Unfortunately, superannuation funds are not eligible to claim a 50 per cent discount.

Real estate

If your super fund were to invest in income-producing property (such as commercial and residential property), your fund would receive a regular income stream (rent) plus capital growth if the property appreciated in value. As a general rule, property in good locations tends to double in value every seven to 10 years. As superannuation is a long-term investment strategy, this class of investment could prove a good way of accumulating benefits that members can access when they retire.

At a glance: benefits of investing in real estate

The benefits your super fund can gain from investing in real estate are:

- *Income (rent).* Rent is normally payable every month. Under Australian tax law, rent is liable to tax when it's paid or credited to your super fund. The average gross rental yield is normally around 4 per cent, and the net yield (after payment of rental expenses and taxation) is generally around 3 per cent.

- *Capital growth.* Real estate is a long-term investment strategy that has the capacity to increase in value. This could prove an excellent way of building up member benefits.

- *Tax benefits.* There are three tax advantages to investing in real estate:

  - *Tax deductions.* Expenditure (such as interest, rates and land taxes, insurance, repairs and depreciation) are tax deductible, and you could qualify for a capital works deduction (building write-off deduction).

  - *CGT discount.* If your super fund makes a capital gain on the sale of a property during the accumulation phase, only two-thirds of the capital gain is assessable, provided the property has been owned for more than 12 months (see chapter 6). The good news gets even better if you sell a property during the super fund's pension phase, as the entire capital gain on sale is then exempt from tax (see chapter 8).

▫ *Small business concessions.* If you operate a small business and sell or transfer your business premises to your SMSF, under the CGT concessions for small business, any capital gain you make on disposal of those assets may be concessionally taxed or exempt from tax (see chapter 4).

■ *No volatility.* Property values tend to be less volatile than the value of shares and tend to rise over the long term.

At a glance: limitations of investing in real estate

The limitations, or risks, of investing in real estate are:

■ *Expensive investment.* The purchase price of a property can vary upwards from $200 000 to well over a few million dollars. So your super fund may not be in a position to buy a property outright. But an SMSF is permitted to borrow money under certain circumstance to purchase a rental property (see chapter 4).

■ *Liquidity problems.* A major risk with real estate is that it is not liquid: it could take months to sell and there's no guarantee you will receive the sale price you're seeking. This could become a major concern if your super fund needs cash immediately to pay retirement benefits to members or a lump sum death benefit to a dependant in the event of a member's death (see chapter 8). The Tax Office has advised that an inability to cash pension assets (such as property) to meet minimum pension payments is a common mistake of SMSFs.

- *Entry and exit fees.* You will incur purchase costs (such as stamp duty imposed by state and territory governments on property purchases) and selling costs (such as an agent's commission to sell the property). Depending on the value of the property, these outlays could amount to many thousands of dollars.

- *Holding costs.* Ongoing costs (such as rates and land taxes, insurance and maintenance costs) must be met whether the property is leased or vacant. This could have an adverse impact on a super fund's cash flow if the property were to become vacant.

- *Lose money.* There's a risk property values could fall or the property could become vacant for a substantial period of time; which could adversely affect member benefits.

Managed funds

Managed funds are mutual investment funds managed by Australia's leading financial institutions. They give small investors (such as SMSFs) the opportunity to invest in a wide range of asset classes that they cannot ordinarily afford to purchase. The minimum you can invest is normally $2000. This is a good way of building up a diversified investment portfolio, and you can select a mix of investment options to suit your particular circumstances. The asset classes you can consider include:

- *Cash.* Your money is invested in securities such as bank bills and government bonds.

- *Equity growth.* Your money is invested in domestic and foreign share markets.

- *Indexed.* Your money is invested in a particular index (such as the S&P/ASX 200 index comprising the top 200 companies and property trusts listed on the ASX).

- *Property.* Your money is invested in major residential, industrial and commercial property developments located throughout Australia or overseas, or both.

When you invest in a managed fund you will buy units. Depending on the investments you select, the value of your units will rise and fall in line with the prevailing market. You can also buy additional units at regular intervals.

At a glance: benefits of investing in managed funds

The benefits your super fund can gain from investing in managed funds are:

- *Income.* Managed funds normally pay at least two income distributions each year.

- *Capital growth.* Your units can increase in value and help build member benefits. This will depend on the performance of the underlying investments you had selected.

- *Tax benefits.* If you invest in shares that pay franked dividends, your fund will benefit from dividend franking credits, and if you invest in property, your fund may receive tax-free distributions.

- *Liquidity.* Your units can be sold quickly and you will normally get your money back within seven days. The amount you receive will depend on the market value of your units at the time of sale.

- *Entry and exit fees.* The cost of buying and selling your units is minimal.

At a glance: limitations of investing in managed funds

The limitations, or risks, of investing in managed funds are:

- *Holding costs.* You will incur ongoing management and administration fees, and you could also have to pay contribution fees and switching fees. The relevant details are set out in the product disclosure statement that you need to read when you join the fund (see chapter 1).

- *Volatility.* Your units will rise and fall in line with the prevailing market, as is the case with shares, and there's a risk that your units could fall in value, which would adversely affect member benefits.

Collectables

An SMSF can invest in certain approved collectables and personal-use assets (such as artwork, jewellery, antiques, classic cars, wine, rare coins and stamps) provided the investment is in accordance with your super fund's investment strategy (see Investment strategy on p. 140). However, a member cannot gain a personal benefit from the purchase of collectables, and the sole purpose of buying them must be to provide retirement benefits for members. This means a trustee cannot display the collectables in their home, nor can a trustee use and enjoy them (for instance, drive a prized classic car or wear jewellery that the super fund owns). For more information, see Tax Office Ruling SMSFR 2008/2: *Self Managed Superannuation Funds: the application of the sole purpose test in section 62 of the* Superannuation Industry (Supervision) Act 1993 *to the provision of benefits other than retirement, employment termination or death benefits.* Generally, you need to have some degree of skill and knowledge regarding what collectables are worth buying, and whether they're likely to appreciate in value. It's best that you seek expert advice if you're not sure, and that you check the collectables you plan to buy do not contravene the SIS Act. Stiff financial penalties may apply if you fail to comply with the various rules and regulations associated with investing in collectable and personal-use assets. And your super fund could be deemed non-compliant if the breaches are found to be serious and lose its tax concessions.

At a glance: benefits of investing in collectables

The benefits your super fund can gain from investing in collectables are:

- *Capital growth.* Certain collectables (such as artwork) have a capacity to increase in value and help build member benefits.

- *Tax benefits.* Under the CGT provisions, capital gains on collectables that cost $500 or less are disregarded, and capital gains on the sale of classic cars are exempt from tax.

At a glance: limitations of investing in collectables

The limitations (risks) of investing in collectables are:

- *Income.* As most collectables must be kept in storage, you will not ordinarily derive an income stream from them.

- *Volatility.* The market value of major collectables rise and fall in line with the prevailing market.

- *Entry and exit fees.* As these items are normally purchased at an auction, you will incur commission fees at the time you buy and sell them. (The commission fees are generally around 10 to 20 per cent of the purchase and sale price.)

- *Liquidity.* Collectables are not a liquid investment. It could take months to sell a collectable and there's no guarantee you will receive the sale price you're seeking. This could become a major concern if your super fund has insufficient cash on hand to meet minimum pension payments. To reduce the risk, it's best that you invest in popular collectables, such as artwork, antiques, classic cars, rare coins and stamps that can be readily sold at auction.

- *Capital losses.* There's a risk that collectables could fall in value. Under the CGT provisions, a capital loss on the sale of a collectable can only be deducted from a capital gain you make on the sale of another collectable.

- *Holding costs.* The federal Labor government has proposed that from 1 July 2011 collectables must be insured and kept in storage, and the trustee must get annual valuations.

 Tax tip

An SMSF can lease collectables to a related party, provided the super fund charges a commercial rental fee, and the market value of the collectables does not exceed 5 per cent of the total market value of the SMSF's assets. For more details see Tax Office Ruling SMSFR 2008/2: *Self Managed Superannuation Funds: the application of the sole purpose test in section 62 of the* Superannuation Industry (Supervision) Act 1993 *to the provision of benefits other than retirement, employment termination or death benefits.*

Useful references

- Department of Families, Community Services and Indigenous Affairs publication: *Investing for your retirement* available from

- Australian Securities & Investments Commission consumer website <www.moneysmart.gov.au>. Go to 'About financial products — Superannuation', and click on 'Choosing your investment strategy'.

Australian Taxation Office interpretative decisions

- ID 2007/56: *Superannuation: Self Managed Superannuation Funds: contracts for differences (CFDs) — no fund assets deposited with CFD provider*

- ID 2007/57: *Superannuation: Self Managed Superannuation Fund: contracts for differences (CFDs) — fund assets deposited with CFD provider — charge over fund assets*

- ID 2007/58: *Superannuation: Self Managed Superannuation Fund: trustee using a margin account for fund investments in listed shares*

- ID 2009/92: *Superannuation income tax: tax treatment of losses realised by a complying SMSF on disposal of shares*

- ID 2010/162: *Superannuation: Self Managed Superannuation Fund: limited recourse borrowing arrangement—borrowing from a related party on terms favourable to the self managed superannuation fund*

Other taxation rulings

- Superannuation Circular 2003/1: *Self managed superannuation funds*

- SMSFR 2008/2: *Self Managed Superannuation Fund: the application of the sole purpose test in section 62 of the* Superannuation Industry (Supervision) Act 1993 *to the provision of benefits other than retirement, employment termination or death benefits*

Chapter 8

Accessing your super fund benefits: enjoying the spoils

The sole purpose of a complying super fund must be to provide benefits to members upon retirement, and benefits to dependants in the event of a member's death. Contributions to a complying super fund are also made to provide benefits to you when you retire, and benefits to dependants in the event of your death. As superannuation is a long-term strategy, the more you're able to accumulate, the more you will have when you can legally access your preserved benefits, which usually occurs when you reach your preservation age and retire. When that historic moment in your life arrives, you have the option to purchase a superannuation pension, take a lump sum payment or receive a combination of both.

As an added bonus, you will also gain significant tax benefits. In this chapter, I discuss when you can legally access your preserved benefits, the various superannuation pension options available, and the tax benefits you can gain.

Conditions of release

Under Australian tax law, you generally cannot access your preserved benefits until you reach your preservation age and satisfy a condition of release.

Preservation age

Your preservation age depends on the date you were born. If you were born before 1960 you can access your preserved benefits once you reach 55 years of age, and if you were born after 1964 you need to wait until you turn 60 (see table 8.1). The most common condition of release is retirement. You will be considered to have retired if you can satisfy the trustee of your super fund that you have no intention of working more than 10 hours per week.

Table 8.1: preservation age

Date of birth	Preservation age
Before 1 July 1960	55 years
1 July 1960 – 30 June 1961	56 years
1 July 1961 – 30 June 1962	57 years

Date of birth	Preservation age
1 July 1962 – 30 June 1963	58 years
1 July 1963 – 30 June 1964	59 years
From 1 July 1964	60 years

At a glance: conditions of release

The main means by which you can access your preserved benefits are summarised below.

- You reach your preservation age and retire. This will depend on the date you were born; contact the trustee(s) of your fund.

- You reach your preservation age (currently 55 years of age) and elect to receive a transition to retirement pension; contact the trustee(s) of your fund.

- You cease your current employment after you reach 60 years of age, and you're no longer contributing to your super fund; contact the trustee(s) of your fund.

- You reach 65 years of age—even if you're still working; contact the trustee(s) of your fund.

- You have less than $200 in preserved benefits and terminate employment; contact the trustee(s) of your fund.

- You become disabled or ill and are unlikely to work again; contact the trustee(s) of your fund.

- You need to access your preserved benefits on compassionate grounds (for instance, for medical reasons, mortgage assistance or funeral assistance); contact the Australian Prudential Regulation Authority (APRA).

- You are experiencing severe financial hardship; contact the Australian Taxation Office (ATO).

- You are a temporary resident permanently leaving Australia; contact the ATO.

- You are terminally ill; contact the trustee(s) of your fund (see chapter 9).

- You die; your next-of-kin should contact the trustee(s) of your fund (see chapter 9).

Severe financial hardship

If you experience severe financial hardship, you may be eligible for early release of your preserved superannuation fund benefits. However, you can only make an application if you satisfy certain conditions:

- *Under your preservation age.* If you're less than 55 years of age you must have been in receipt of Commonwealth income support for the past 26 weeks, and also be able to demonstrate that you're unable to meet 'reasonable and immediate living expenses'. For example, you have insufficient funds to pay for overdue household bills, such as rent, gas, electricity, telephone and credit cards. If your superannuation fund approves your application, the trustee may release during a particular financial year a lump sum payment of between $1000 and $10 000, or the entire amount if you have less than $1000 in your account.

- *Over your preservation age.* You must have been in receipt of Commonwealth income support for the past 39 weeks and not be gainfully employed either full time or part time. If your superannuation fund approves your application, the trustee may release your entire benefit to you.

For more details you can visit the Australian Prudential Regulation Authority (APRA) website <www.apra.gov.au> and go to 'Other grounds for early release of super-annuation benefits'.

Temporary resident

If you hold an eligible temporary resident visa that has expired or been cancelled and you permanently leave Australia, you can claim your superannuation benefits while you were working in Australia (referred to as departing Australia superannuation payments). These payments are ordinarily liable to 35 per cent withholding tax, which is payable before you leave. For more details see the Tax Office publication *Working temporarily in Australia—claim your superannuation after you leave* (NAT 8592).

Pensions

On 1 July 2007 the federal government introduced a number of tax incentives to encourage Australians to take a superannuation pension rather than withdraw their benefits in cash.

At a glance: SMSFs and starting a pension

The key conditions and procedures to start a superannuation pension are as follows:

- The member must lodge a formal notification and proof with the trustee(s) that they have met a condition of release. The member must specify the pension option they want and the amount to be transferred to a pension fund. Note that an SMSF can only pay a transition to retirement pension or account-based pension (see Buying a superannuation pension on p. 181).

- The trustee(s) prepares minutes confirming the notification and checks whether the super fund's trust deed permits payment of the pension option to the member.

- The relevant member's super fund benefits convert from the accumulation phase to the pension phase, in which earnings are no longer liable to tax.

- The trustee(s) identifies the assets that will fund pension payments. The trustee(s) must obtain an annual actuarial report if the pension assets are not segregated. (The actuarial report verifies the market value of the assets that fund the pension payments.)

- The trustee(s) prepares a product disclosure statement (PDS) setting out the assets that back the fund pension payments, payment details and tax payable if the member is aged less than 60.

- The trustee(s) withholds pay-as-you-go (PAYG) withholding tax for the taxable component of pension if the member is less than age 60 (less the 15 per cent tax offset). (See chapter 8.)

- The trustee(s) notifies the member that the pension has been approved and details of payment. Pension must be paid in cash. For payments by cheque see Tax Office Ruling SMSFR 2010/D1: *Self managed superannuation funds: the scope and operation of subparagraph 17A(3)(b)(ii) of the* Superannuation Industry (Supervision) Act 1993.

- The trustee(s) must pay an annual minimum pension each year for a transition to retirement pension or account-based pension (see Buying a superannuation pension on p. 181).

Taxation

If you purchase a superannuation pension from a complying superannuation fund with your preserved benefits, the amount of tax payable depends on whether you're under or over 60 years of age, and the payment's classification (see figure 8.1). The Tax Office calls a superannuation pension a superannuation income stream. Your preserved benefits may consist of a combination of tax-free components and taxable components. This is to take into account the old rules of taxing super funds and contributions before 30 June 1983 (pre-1983), and the new tax rules that apply to taxing super funds and certain contributions made after 1 July 1983 (post-1983). These components are taxed as follows.

Tax-free component

These payments are tax free and are excluded from your assessable income. They can be made up of the following:

- pre–1 July 1983 component (if you commenced employment before 1 July 1983)

- concessional component (see chapter 5)

- post-1994 invalidity component

- CGT-exempt amount component (see chapter 5)

- non-concessional contributions component (see chapter 5).

Taxable component—taxed element

These are post–July 1983 accumulated benefits in a complying super fund that was liable to a 15 per cent tax rate (such as employer contributions, pre-tax concessional contributions and investment earnings).

Figure 8.1: taxing a superannuation income stream

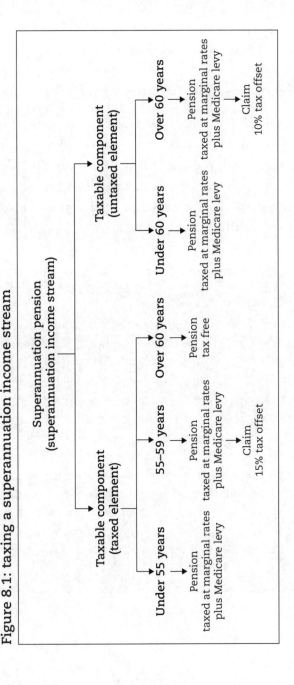

These payments are liable to tax, but are tax free once you turn 60 years of age (see figure 8.1).

Taxable component—untaxed element

These are post–July 1983 accumulated benefits in a superannuation fund that haven't been taxed. These payments will ordinarily come from certain federal and state government super schemes that don't pay tax, and proceeds of a life insurance policy that are not taxed when they're distributed (see figure 8.1).

Tax tip

If you have a taxable component in your super fund and satisfy a condition of release (for instance, retired), consider the option of withdrawing your benefits and making a re-contribution back into your super fund. If you do this, your benefits will become a tax-free component. This will benefit your beneficiaries in the event of your death. This is because no tax is payable when superannuation death benefit payments containing a tax-free component are distributed to dependants (see chapter 9). A financial planner can help you with this strategy. For the Tax Office views on this strategy, see *Superannuation Technical Sub-committee minutes*—5 June 2007.

Tax tip

Before 1 July 1983 a superannuation lump sum payment (pre–July 1983 component) was liable to tax at the rate of 5 per cent. That's why the government changed the rules on 1 July 1983; it was apparently too generous!

Receiving a superannuation pension

This section describes how you will be taxed if you receive a superannuation pension (or superannuation income stream).

Under 55 years of age

If you can access your preserved benefits before you turn 55 years of age (for instance, because you are incapacitated), your pension payments are liable to tax at your marginal rates, plus a Medicare levy (see figure 8.1 on p. 177). This can very between 0 per cent and 46.5 per cent; see appendix A, table 1.

Between 55 and 59 years of age

If you are aged between 55 and 59 years, the taxable component—taxed element part of your pension payment is taxed at your marginal rates, plus a Medicare levy. As the pension is paid from a taxed source (your super fund), you can claim a 15 per cent tax offset (see figure 8.1) on these payments when you do your income tax return each year.

For example, if you receive a $50 000 pension, you can claim a $7500 tax offset ($50 000 × 15 per cent = $7500), which you can offset against the tax payable on the taxable income you derive. Any unused tax offsets cannot be refunded back to you (as is the case if you receive a dividend franking credit). The good news here is when your superannuation fund is in the pension phase, all investment income and capital gains your fund derives from the assets that fund your pension payments are exempt from tax.

On the other hand, the taxable component—untaxed element part of your pension payment is taxed at your marginal rates, plus a Medicare levy. In this case, you will miss out on claiming the 15 per cent tax offset, as the pension payments are coming from a super fund that doesn't pay tax. This will ordinarily be the case if you're a government employee (see figure 8.1 on p. 177).

Over 60 years of age

Once you reach 60 years of age all pension payments and cash withdrawals from a complying superannuation fund are tax free. To add icing to the exemption cake, the pension is also excluded from your assessable income. This means that if the superannuation pension is your sole source of income; your taxable income is effectively nil. On the other hand, if you receive a pension from a super fund that doesn't pay tax (such as certain federal and state government super schemes), the pension is taxed at your marginal rates, plus a Medicare levy. Your super fund may deduct PAYG withholding tax from your pension payments. To help ease the pain you can claim a 10 per cent tax offset (see figure 8.1 on p. 177).

 Tax trap

Once your super fund is in the pension phase, you can't make any further payments to help boost pension payments. If you have surplus funds, you can start up a new pension account.

Buying a superannuation pension

There are three different types of superannuation pensions (or superannuation income streams, in the Tax Office's terminology) that you can purchase from a complying super fund with your accumulated benefits. Each pension option will have certain features that may or may not interest you. The three pensions you can select are:

- transition to retirement pension
- account-based pension
- non–account based pension (or life pension).

 Tax tip

There's no obligation to withdraw your benefits when you retire. However, it's best to start a pension when you reach 60 years of age, because

> **Tax tip** *(cont'd)*
>
> any investment earnings derived during the pension phase are exempt from tax. The trade-off here is that you must withdraw a minimum tax-free pension each year. If you're less than 65 years of age, the amount is 4 per cent of your account balance (see figure 8.2 on p. 195 for minimum superannuation payment percentages).

Transition to retirement pension

A transition to retirement pension is an account-based pension that allows a member to receive a pension (or superannuation income stream), and remain working either full time or part time. This is a kind of account-based pension because the pension payments are based on investment performance and the amount of benefits you have in your account. You need to satisfy a number of conditions if you want to receive a transition to retirement pension. The main ones are as follows:

- You must reach your preservation age, currently 55 years of age if you're born before 1960, at the time you apply for this pension.

- You must elect to receive a non-commutable pension. This means your accumulated benefits in your pension fund can't be converted into a lump sum payment until you reach 65 years of age or retire before 65.

- The amount of pension you can receive each year must fall between 4 per cent and 10 per cent of the balance in your super fund pension account. For instance, if your accumulated benefits are $350 000, you can receive a pension that falls between $14 000 and $35 000. The pension is recalculated at the beginning of each financial year.

- You can't make any further contributions to your pension account once it's set up. If you want to go on contributing to super, you can do this in a new superannuation account.

If you're between 55 and 59 years of age at the time you receive a transition to retirement pension, PAYG withholding tax is deducted from the taxable component of your pension. But you will qualify for a 15 per cent tax offset. For instance, if the pension you receive is $35 000 you can claim a $5250 tax offset ($35 000 × 15 per cent = $5250). But once you reach 60 years of age, the entire pension is tax free and excluded from your assessable income. In the meantime, all the investment income and capital gains your pension fund account derives during the pension phase are exempt from tax. If you run an SMSF you can select the investment assets to fund your pension payments (such as a quality share portfolio).

The great thing about this pension option is your capacity to access your preserved benefits once you reach your preservation age (currently age 55) while still gainfully employed. It also gives you the flexibility to increase the amount of income you're currently earning, or reduce your working hours if you want to work part time. Once you reach 55 years of age, you may qualify for a $500 mature age tax offset if you're still gainfully employed and your income from working is between $10 000 and $53 000. Meanwhile, you can continue to make super contributions (such as salary sacrifice contributions) up to your cap amount into your super fund's accumulation account, which you can access at a later date (see chapter 5).

Case study: transition to retirement pension

Gregory is 59 years of age and has a $500 000 balance in his complying superannuation fund. He's keen to receive a pension and now wants to work part time. Because Gregory has reached his preservation age he can take a transition to retirement pension. According to the rules, Gregory needs to take a pension that falls between $20 000 per annum ($500 000 × 4 per cent = $20 000) and $50 000 per annum ($500 000 × 10 per cent = $50 000). He has elected to receive the maximum pension permitted namely $50 000. This pension is liable to tax at his marginal rates, plus a Medicare levy. As he is less than 60 years of age, he will qualify for a $7500 tax offset ($50 000 × 15 per cent = $7500). But once Gregory turns 60 years of age, the entire pension is tax free and excluded from his assessable income. Further, the investment earnings his pension fund derives to fund his pension payments are also exempt from tax. Meanwhile, Gregory has elected to make a $10 000 salary sacrifice contribution from his part-time salary, which he will be able to access when he permanently retires. Because Gregory is over 55 years of age he will qualify for a $500 mature age tax offset in respect of the salary he's deriving.

Account-based pension

An account-based pension is similar to a transition to retirement pension, in which your benefits are invested on your behalf to fund your annual pension payments. To qualify for this pension you need to reach your preservation age and satisfy a condition of release, such as retire. You also need to transfer your unrestricted non-preserved benefits (benefits that you can now access immediately) to a pension fund account. All investment income and capital gains your pension fund derives from the assets backing your pension are exempt from tax. If you're between 55 and 59 years of age, the pension qualifies for a 15 per cent tax offset. For instance, if you receive a $40 000 pension you can claim a $6000 tax offset ($40 000 × 15 per cent = $6000). But when you reach 60 years of age the entire pension is tax free and excluded from your assessable income.

What makes this an attractive pension option is your capacity to vary the pension payments each year, and the pension will continue to be paid until all your funds are diminished. This will depend on the amount you withdraw each year and the performance of the investments you had selected to fund your pension payments. No payment is required if you commence the pension between 1 June and 30 June. The pension is recalculated at the beginning of each financial year and there are no maximum withdrawal limits to restrict how much you can take out, which means you can effectively withdraw the entire amount. However, if you're less than 60 years of age the taxable component of lump sum withdrawals is liable to tax (see the section Lump sum withdrawals on p. 192). In the event of your death, the pension can continue to be paid to your nominated beneficiaries (such as your spouse) until all the funds are used up, or you can have a lump sum balance paid to your estate (see chapter 9). To ensure that your instructions will be followed, it's best that you prepare a binding death benefit nomination (see chapters 1 and 9).

But as they say in the small print, conditions apply! There are a number of rules you need to comply with if you want to receive an account-based pension. The main ones are:

- You must satisfy a condition of release (such as retire).

- You must invest a prescribed minimum to fund the pension (for instance, $20 000)

- The pension must be paid to you annually (though it is normally payable fortnightly).

- You must receive a prescribed minimum, which can vary depending on your age, between 4 per cent and 14 per cent of your account balance (see table 8.2, overleaf). For instance, if you're under 65 years of age you must withdraw at least 4 per cent of your account balance, and if you're 95 years and over, 14 per cent. (For financial years ended 30 June 2009 to 30 June 2011 inclusive, the prescribed minimum was reduced by 50 per cent for each age group. It was announced in the 2011–12 federal budget that a drawdown concession of 25 per cent will apply until 30 June 2012).

- Once you set up the pension fund you can't make any further contributions to that account. If you still have benefits in your accumulation account or in another super fund, you can set up a second pension fund.

- If you're less than 60 years of age, PAYG withholding tax is deducted from the taxable component of your pension.

A major risk with account-based pensions is your benefits can quickly diminish if the asset classes you chose to fund your pension payments were to decrease significantly in value (for instance, a share portfolio). If this were to occur your pension payments will decrease. It's best that you invest your money wisely (see chapter 7).

Table 8.2: minimum superannuation pension payments from 2012

Age	30 June 2013 and after	30 June 2012
Under 65	4 per cent	3.0 per cent
65–74	5 per cent	3.75 per cent
75–79	6 per cent	4.5 per cent
80–84	7 per cent	5.25 per cent
85–89	9 per cent	6.75 per cent
90–94	11 per cent	8.25 per cent
95 and over	14 per cent	10.5 per cent

Note: For the financial years ended 30 June 2009 to 2011 inclusive, the federal government reduced the minimum withdrawal requirements by 50 per cent for each age group. It was announced in the 2011–12 federal budget that a drawdown concession of 25 per cent will apply until 30 June 2012.

 Tax trap

In the event of the death of a member, an SMSF cannot pay an account-based pension to a person who is not a dependant. Account-based pensions can be paid only to a dependant beneficiary (see chapter 9).

Case study: account-based pension

Christine is 57 years old, has $800 000 in her SMSF and wants to retire early. As she has reached her preservation age and satisfied a condition of release (retirement), she has elected to receive an account-based pension. As Christine is under 65 years of age, the minimum superannuation pension she must receive is $32000 per annum (4 per cent of her account balance) ($800000 × 4 per cent = $32000) (see table 8.2). For this financial year she has elected to receive a $40000 pension, which is recalculated at the beginning of each financial year. As her superannuation fund is now in the pension phase, all investment income and capital gains derived to fund her pension payments are exempt from tax. As Christine is between 55 and 59 years of age, the pension is liable to tax at her marginal rates plus a Medicare levy, but she will qualify for a $6000 tax offset ($40000 × 15 per cent = $6000). Once Christine turns 60 years of age the entire pension is exempt from tax and excluded from her assessable income.

 Tax trap

If your superannuation fund's asset to fund pension payments is a rental property, there's a risk the fund may not be in a position to pay pensions to members. This could happen if the minimum pension payment is more than the net rent received, for instance. This is a common mistake for SMSFs (see chapter 4).

Non–account based pension

Non–account based pensions are normally lifetime pensions that you can purchase with your accumulated superannuation fund benefits. The pension can also be paid over a guaranteed period of time, such as 20 years. For instance, if the agreed pension amount is $40 000 per annum, you will be assured of getting this amount each year over the guaranteed period of time. The good news here is that if the investments used to fund your pension payments were to decrease in value, the super fund bears all the risk. This is great to know if you want this type of security. Unfortunately, this is not the case if you receive an account-based pension. Only industry funds, retail funds and government funds can offer this pension option to you. If you run an SMSF and want a non–account based pension, you will need to transfer your benefits to an industry fund or retail fund.

As is the case with all superannuation income streams, if you're between 55 and 59 years of age the pension qualifies for a 15 per cent tax offset. For instance, if you receive a $40 000 pension you can claim a $6000 tax offset ($40 000 × 15 per cent = $6000). But when you reach 60 years of age the entire pension is tax free and excluded from your assessable income.

Although you're guaranteed an agreed pension amount each year, there are a number of limitations that you need to be aware of. The main ones are:

- You can't vary your pension payments each year (except for inflation). You can only increase your pension payments each year to counter the impact of inflation (for instance, in line with the consumer price index, or CPI — the index that Australia uses to measure the rate of inflation).

- You can't withdraw lump sum payments as you can with an account-based pension.

- You can't commute (change) your pension back into a lump sum.

- If you die shortly after the pension commences your beneficiaries may not be entitled to receive any benefits from this pension scheme. If you're in poor heath a non–account based pension may not be the way to go.

 Tax trap

An SMSF is ineligible to pay a non–account based pension to its members.

Case study: non–account based pension

Harry is 57 years of age and in good health. He has $800 000 in his super fund and wants to retire early. As Harry has reached his preservation age and satisfied a condition of release (retirement), he has elected to receive a non–account based pension. He has done this because he likes the idea that the pension will be guaranteed for the rest of his life. In exchange for his $800 000 lump sum amount, he will receive a $40 000 pension each year. According to the superannuation rules, the pension can only increase each year to counter the impact of inflation, and it cannot be commuted back into a lump sum. As Harry is between 55 and 59 years of age, the pension is liable to tax at his marginal rates plus a Medicare levy, but he will qualify for a $6000 tax offset ($40 000 × 15 per cent = $6000). Once Harry turns 60 years of age the entire pension is exempt from tax and excluded from his assessable income.

Lump sum withdrawals

If you receive a lump sum payment from a complying superannuation fund you will be taxed as follows.

Under preservation age

If you have not reached your preservation age and are eligible to receive a superannuation lump sum payment, you will be taxed as outlined here:

- *Taxable component (taxed element).* The entire amount is taxed at the rate of 21.5 per cent.

- *Taxable component (untaxed element).* This is taxed at two different rates:

◻ Amounts up to the untaxed-plan cap amount (UPCA), which is $1 205 000 for the 2011–12 financial year, are taxed at the rate of 31.5 per cent.

◻ Amounts above the UPCA are taxed at the rate of 46.5 per cent (see figure 8.2).

Preservation age to 59 years of age

If you're between your preservation age and 59 years of age and you receive a superannuation lump sum payment, you will be taxed as follows:

■ *Taxable component (taxed element).* This is taxed at two different rates:

◻ Amounts up to the low rate cap amount (LRCA), which is $165 000 for the 2011–12 financial year, are tax free.

◻ Amounts above the LRCA are taxed at the rate of 16.5 per cent.

■ *Taxable component (untaxed element).* This is taxed at three different rates:

◻ Amounts up to the LRCA are taxed at the rate of 16.5 per cent.

◻ Amounts between the LRCA and the UPCA are taxed at the rate of 31.5 per cent.

◻ Amounts above the UPCA are taxed at the rate of 46.5 per cent (see figure 8.2 on p. 195).

Over 60 years of age

If you're over 60 years of age and eligible to receive a superannuation lump sum payment, you will be taxed as follows:

- *Taxable component (taxed element)*. The entire amount you receive is tax free.

- *Taxable component (untaxed element)*:

  ▫ Amounts up to the UPCA are taxed at the rate of 16.5 per cent.

  ▫ Amounts above the UPCA are taxed at the rate of 46.5 per cent (see figure 8.2).

 Tax tip

As superannuation fund benefits are made up of a combination of tax-free components and taxable components, when you withdraw money from your super fund, you need to withdraw a combination of any tax-free components and taxable components in proportion (ratio) to the total amount held in your super fund. Unfortunately, you can't nominate the relevant component. For instance, if 25 per cent of your benefits consists of tax-free components, 25 per cent of any withdrawals you make must come from this source. You need to do this because, in the event of your death, your beneficiaries are liable to pay tax on any taxable component that is held in your superannuation fund.

Figure 8.2: superannuation lump sum payments

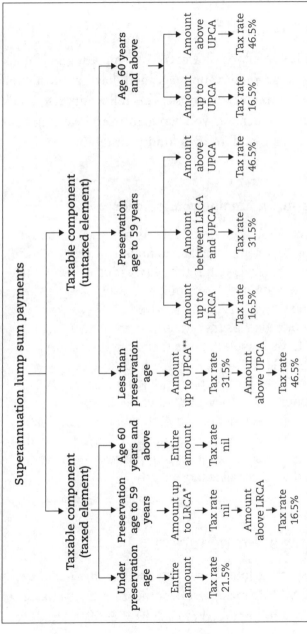

Note: Tax rates include 1.5% Medicare levy

*LRCA = low rate cap amount

**UPCA = untaxed plan cap amount

Receiving a super pension from an SMSF

Setting up an SMSF is worth contemplating if you are nearing your preservation age and have a substantial amount of money to invest. The following case study illustrates the benefits you can gain from investing your money in an SMSF to help fund your retirement.

Case study: funding your pension

John and Betty are both 59 years of age. They do not belong to a complying superannuation fund and are keen to retire when they turn 60 years of age. On 1 June they sold an investment property they jointly owned and now have $1200000 to invest. If they invest the funds outside the super system, the investment income they derive is liable to tax at their marginal rates, plus a Medicare levy. So they don't have to pay tax, they have been advised to set up an SMSF (see chapter 3). This is because once they turn 60 years of age and retire, all pension payments and cash withdrawals payable from a complying superannuation fund during the pension phase are exempt from tax and are excluded from their assessable income.

Making a contribution

The first thing John and Betty need to do after they set up an SMSF is make a superannuation contribution to get the ball rolling. As they each have $600000 to invest, there are restrictions on the amount they can contribute to a superannuation fund each financial year. If they breach the contributions cap amount, the excess amount is taxed at the rate of 46.5 per cent (see chapter 5).

To do this by the book, John and Betty need to make two contributions. They were advised to make a $150 000 personal after-tax, or non-concessional, contribution before the end of the current financial year (A), and a further $450 000 at the beginning of the next financial year (B). Under Australian tax law, as they are under 65 years of age, both John and Betty can make a one-off $450 000 non-concessional contribution during the financial year (B). However, if they do this they're ineligible to make any further non-concessional contribution in the following two financial years (see chapter 5). That's why they each need to contribute $150 000 at the outset and $450 000 in the following year. These contributions come from an after-tax source, so no 15 per cent contributions tax is payable, as these payments do not qualify for a tax deduction.

Investment strategy

To spread their risk John's investment strategy is to invest his $600 000 in a quality share portfolio paying 5 per cent fully franked dividends, while Betty's strategy is to invest in a term deposit paying a 6 per cent rate of interest. The benefits John and Betty will gain from investing in a superannuation fund (and, more particularly, an SMSF) are set out in the following case studies.

Case study: John

The details of John's investment strategy (shares) and payments are shown in table 8.3.

Table 8.3: John's investment strategy and payments

Investment	Amount
Capital	$600 000
Investment allocation	Shares (paying fully franked dividends)
Earnings rate	5 per cent
Annual earnings	$42 857 (consisting of dividends and dividend franking credits)
Tax payable	Nil
Administration costs	$1000
Net earnings	$41 857

Here are the essential features of John's pension:

⇒ Dividends and franking credits and capital gains on the sale of shares derived during the pension phase to fund John's pension are tax free.

⇒ As John's pension fund is exempt of tax, all dividend franking credits are refunded back to the pension fund.

⇒ John can withdraw a $41 857 tax-free pension each year based on the pension's earnings, which is excluded from his assessable income, without having to draw down any of his capital.

⇒ John can earn a further $16000 outside the super scheme before he is liable to pay tax, given that he can claim a low-income tax offset; see appendix A, table 3.

Case study: Betty

The details of Betty's investment strategy (term deposit) and payments are shown in table 8.4.

Table 8.4: Betty's investment strategy and payments

Investment	Amount
Capital	$600000
Investment allocation	Term deposit
Interest rate	6 per cent
Interest derived	$36000
Tax payable	Nil
Administration costs	$1000
Net earnings	$35000

Here are the essential features of Betty's pension:

⇒ Interest derived during the pension phase to fund Betty's pension is exempt from tax.

⇒ Betty can withdraw a $35 000 tax-free pension each year based on the pension's earnings, which is excluded from her assessable income, without having to draw down any of her capital.

⇒ Betty can earn a further $16 000 outside the super scheme before she's liable to pay tax, given that she can claim a low-income tax offset; see appendix A, table 3.

Useful references

■ Australian Prudential Regulation Authority (APRA) publication: *Early release of superannuation: information on accessing your superannuation before retirement age*

Australian Taxation Office publications

■ *Changes to pension standards for self-managed super funds*

■ *Self-managed super funds and tax exemptions on pension assets*

■ *Transition to retirement* (NAT 14967)

Other taxation rulings

■ TA 2009/1: *Superannuation illegal early release arrangements*

CHAPTER 9

Death and taxes: superannuation death benefits

One of the major conditions for contributing to a complying superannuation fund, and more particularly an SMSF, is to provide benefits to dependants in the event of a member's death. The trustee(s) can pay either a superannuation income stream (pension) or a lump sum death benefit to dependants. How your beneficiaries are taxed depends on whether they are dependants or non-dependants, and whether they receive a pension or lump sum. In this chapter, I discuss the taxation issues associated with the payment of superannuation death benefits to your beneficiaries.

Dependants and non-dependants

The taxation of superannuation death benefits depends on whether the beneficiaries you have nominated to receive your super are dependants or non-dependants. Under Australian tax law the following beneficiaries are dependants (also described as SIS dependants) for the purposes of receiving a superannuation death benefit:

- spouse, including a de facto spouse

- former spouse or de facto spouse

- child less than 18 years of age

- a person who is financially dependent on the deceased (at date of death)

- a person who is in an interdependency relationship (at the time of death). According to the Tax Office, an interdependency relationship exists between two people where:

  - they have a close personal relationship, and

  - they live together, even if they are not related by family, and

  - one or each of them provides the other with financial and domestic support and personal care.

If the nominated person does not fall within the definition of a dependant, they will be classified as a non-dependant.

Binding death benefit nomination

If you want your superannuation death benefits to be paid to a specific dependant (or to your estate), you need to fill in a binding death benefit nomination form. You can get this form from your super fund. If you run an SMSF it's best that you give this form to a member. If you give your fund a properly completed form and it's kept up to date, the trustee *must* comply with your instructions, and will have *no discretion* as to how the death benefits should be distributed. This form has to be witnessed, and to remain valid you must renew this legal document every three years.

If you do not make a binding death benefit nomination, the trustee will ordinarily make a payment to the relevant beneficiaries you nominated when you first joined the fund (and the name of your preferred beneficiary is shown every year in your member benefit statement, as described in chapter 1; though you can change the nomination at any time). However, the trustee is not technically obliged to make a payment to the beneficiary you have nominated. Your nomination is used only as a guide as to who should receive your death benefits. To reduce the risk of your benefit *not* going to the person you prefer it's best to prepare a binding death benefit nomination form; see appendix B, Self managed superannuation funds (death benefit payments). For instance, you want your benefits to be paid to your spouse rather than to another dependant who may also be entitled to receive your benefits. Under these circumstances the trustee must comply with your request.

 Tax tip

If you're eligible to access your preserved benefits because of a terminal medical condition (where you're likely to die within 12 months), your benefits are exempt from tax. Two medical practitioners will need to certify that this is the case. For more details see the Tax Office publication *Accessing your super if you have a terminal medical condition*.

Superannuation death benefit pensions

The Tax Office describes pensions as income streams. If you are receiving a superannuation pension at the time of your death, your pension can continue to be paid as a superannuation income stream benefit to what's known as a reversionary beneficiary. A reversionary beneficiary is a dependant who is eligible to receive your pension in the event of your death (and it cannot be paid to your estate). The following beneficiaries are dependants and eligible to be a reversionary beneficiary:

- spouse, de facto spouse, former spouse

- child less than 18 years of age

- a person who is financially dependent on the deceased (at the date of death)

- a person who is in an interdependency relationship (at the date of death).

In chapter 8 I pointed out that when you receive a payment from a complying superannuation fund, it may consist of a combination of three components. This is to take into account the way superannuation funds and contributions were taxed before 30 June 1983, and how certain contributions have been taxed since 1 July 1983. These components are:

- *Tax-free components.* These payments are tax free and are excluded from your assessable income. They include non-concessional contributions and other contributions, such as pre-1983 accumulated amounts and CGT-exempt components (see chapter 8).

- *Taxable component—taxed element.* These are post–July 1983 accumulated benefits in a complying super fund that was liable to tax, such as employer contributions, pre-tax concessional contributions and investment earnings (see chapter 8).

- *Taxable component—untaxed element.* These are post–July 1983 accumulated benefits in a superannuation fund that haven't been taxed. These payments normally come from certain federal and state government super schemes that don't pay tax, and proceeds of a life insurance policy that are not taxed when they're distributed (see chapter 8).

If your beneficiary is a dependant child, your pension can continue to be paid to them until they turn 18 years of age. It will then become a tax-free superannuation lump sum death benefit payment. If your dependant child is permanently disabled, the pension can continue to be paid after they turn 18 until all the funds are consumed. The amount of tax payable on the death benefit you leave depends on your age at the date of your death and the age of your dependant (see figure 9.1).

 Tax tip

A death benefit payment arising from a life insurance policy in the event of a member's death is treated as a payment from an untaxed source (and more particularly a taxable component—untaxed element).

 Tax trap

Under Australian tax law a non-dependant cannot receive your superannuation fund pension in the event of your death. A non-dependant is only eligible to receive a lump sum payment, on which they will pay tax according to a formula.

Figure 9.1: superannuation death benefit income stream

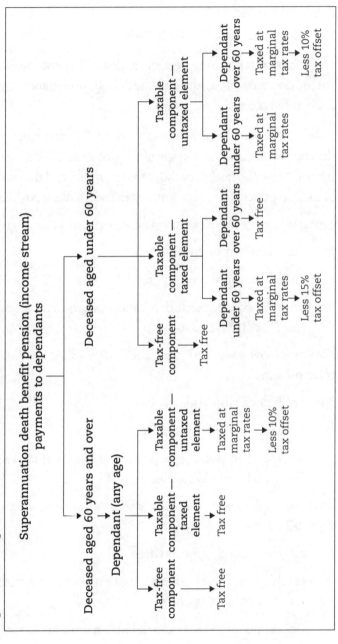

At a glance: how superannuation death benefit pensions are taxed

Only dependants may receive a death benefit pension (income stream, according to the ATO); non-dependants may only receive a lump sum.

How death benefit pensions are taxed in the hands of dependants depends on the age of the deceased and the age of the dependant at the date of the member's death, and the nature of the components (taxed or untaxed elements) of the payment:

Deceased aged over 60 years and a dependant at any age

- tax-free component: tax free

- taxable component: tax free

- untaxed component: dependant's marginal tax rates less 10 per cent tax offset.

Deceased aged under 60 years and a dependant aged more than 60 years

- tax-free component: tax free

- taxable component: tax free

- untaxed component: dependant's marginal tax rates less 10 per cent tax offset.

Deceased aged under 60 years and a dependant aged less than 60 years

- tax-free component: tax free

- taxable component: dependant's marginal tax rates less 15 per cent tax offset

- untaxed component: dependant's marginal tax rates.

Superannuation lump sum death benefits

If your beneficiaries are eligible to receive a lump sum death benefit in the event of your death, the taxation treatment depends on whether the benefit is paid to a dependant or non-dependant, and whether the payment is from a tax-free component or taxable component (taxed element or untaxed element). Non-dependants can only be paid a lump sum death benefit (see figure 9.2, overleaf), though dependants can choose whether they would rather receive a lump sum or a pension from the trustee.

 Tax tip

The Tax Office has advised if an SMSF increases a lump sum death benefit payment to a spouse or child, the fund can claim a tax deduction. The ATO says: 'The deduction is calculated by reference to the increase in the death benefit to allow for tax previously paid by the fund in respect of the deceased member's account'. However the recipient must claim the tax deduction *in the year in which the lump sum death benefit is paid*. For more details see the Tax Office publications *SMSF Newsletter*, Edition 14, and *Super funds and taxation: working together for effective compliance* on the ATO website <www.ato.gov.au>.

Figure 9.2: superannuation death benefit lump sum payments

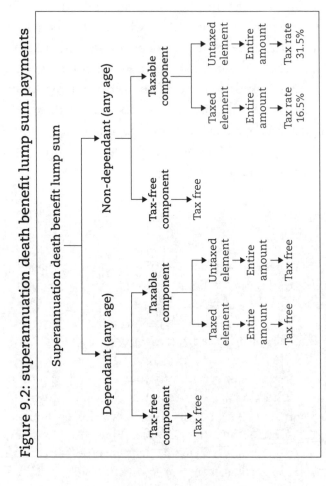

Note: Tax rate includes 1.5% Medicare levy

Tax tip

If beneficiaries are unhappy with a decision the trustees have made over payments of death benefits and they cannot settle the dispute, the matter can be referred to the Superannuation Complaints Tribunal for a resolution (see chapter 1). However, members of an SMSF are ineligible to use this tribunal to resolve disputes arising between the trustees of an SMSF. If any disputes were to arise you will need to refer the matter to the courts for a resolution.

At a glance: how superannuation lump sum death benefits are taxed

Death benefit lump sums are tax free when they are paid to dependants. On the other hand lump sums paid to non-dependants are taxed as follows:

Deceased at any age and non-dependant at any age

- tax-free component: tax free

- taxable component:

  - taxed element: 16.5 per cent

  - untaxed element: 31.5 per cent

Update your legal documents

In conclusion, if you're in receipt of a superannuation pension you should regularly review and update your legal documents (for instance, a binding death benefit nomination and your will) that set out who should receive your pension in the event of your death. This is because your circumstances can quickly change (for instance, your spouse could die or you could get divorced or remarry). Further, beneficiaries who were originally considered dependants under Australian income tax law may now be ineligible (for instance, children over 18 years of age who are no longer classified as dependants). Otherwise, family disputes could arise if your instructions are not clear and precise, and it could be costly if the matter has to be referred to the courts for a resolution.

Useful references

- Australian Securities & Investments Commission consumer website <www.moneysmart.gov.au>. Go to 'About financial products—Superannuation' and click on 'Accessing superannuation death benefits'.

Australian Taxation Office publications

- *Guide to deceased estates*
- *Managing the tax affairs of someone who has died*
- *Paying an income stream death benefit*
- *Paying a lump sum death benefit*
- *Understanding a death benefit paid from a super fund*

Glossary

accumulation phase A period of time in which a complying super fund can accept contributions from its members. The cash your super fund is building up for you is invested on your behalf, and cannot be accessed until you satisfy a condition of release such as retiring. Investment earnings derived during the accumulation phase are liable to a 15 per cent tax rate.

active asset An asset, such as your business premises or factory, that you use to derive assessable income. If you operate a small business and make a capital gain on the sale of an active asset, the capital gain can be reduced to nil.

account-based pension   A superannuation pension in which you can vary the payments each year and which continues to pay you until your funds are exhausted. You must receive a prescribed minimum payment each year, which can vary between 4 per cent and 14 per cent of your account balance.

age pension   A federal government-funded pension payable to Australian residents who have reached the age pension age. The age pension age is set to increase in stages to age 67 by 2022–23. You also need to satisfy a strict income test and asset test to qualify for this pension.

allowable deduction   An expense you can deduct from your assessable income.

approved auditor   A qualified accountant who is authorised to audit a self-managed superannuation fund.

assessable income   Assessable income is ordinary income and statutory income (for instance, capital gains) that are liable to tax.

Australian resident   A person who ordinarily resides in Australia. There are statutory tests to check whether you are a resident of Australia.

Australian Securities Exchange (ASX)   Australia's major securities exchange responsible for regulating and controlling the buying and selling of Australian listed securities, such as shares.

Australian Taxation Office (ATO)   The federal government authority that's responsible for administering the *Income Tax Assessment Act 1997*.

bank bills   A short-term investment with a bank that you purchase at a discount to its face value. When the investment matures you are paid its face value.

binding death benefit nomination   A written request to be prepared if you want your super fund death benefits to be paid to specific beneficiaries or to your estate. The trustee of your super fund must follow your instructions and has no discretion to vary your decision. You must renew this request every three years for it to remain valid. You should also update it whenever your circumstances change, such as through marriage or divorce.

business real property   A business premises (such as a shop, office or factory) that you use to derive your assessable income.

call option   A security that gives the holder the right, but not the obligation, to buy the underlying shares at an agreed price on or before the expiry date. A call option is worth buying in a rising market.

capital gain   A gain you make when you sell a capital gains tax (CGT) asset for a price greater than its cost base. Under Australian income tax law, a capital gain is liable to tax.

capital loss   A loss you incur when you sell a CGT asset for a price below its reduced cost price. Under Australian income tax law, a capital loss can be applied only against a capital gain, but a loss can be carried forward from year to year if there is no gain in the year the loss is incurred.

capital gains tax (CGT)   A tax on gains you make when you dispose of CGT assets, such as shares, real estate and collectables.

capital growth   An increase in the value of particular asset classes, such as units in managed funds, shares, real estate and collectables.

capital proceeds   The sale price of CGT assets, such as shares, property and units in managed funds.

capital works deduction   A specific tax deduction you can claim for the construction costs of an income-producing property, or any improvements or extensions you make to an income-producing property.

certificate of title   A legal document setting out the description of a property and verifying that you're the legal owner of that property.

CGT asset   An asset, such as shares and property, that's liable to tax under the CGT provisions.

collectables   Investment assets (such as artwork, antiques, rare coins and stamps) that a self-managed super fund can invest in. Collectables must be insured and kept in storage and members cannot gain a personal benefit from collectables (such as use or enjoy them).

complying superannuation fund   A fund that has made an election to be regulated under the *Superannuation Industry (Supervision) Act 1993*. Complying super funds are taxed at the rate of 15 per cent and can pay pensions to their members.

concessional contribution   A pre-tax contribution you make to a complying super fund that qualifies for a tax deduction. These contributions are liable to a 15 per cent contributions tax.

concessional contributions cap   The maximum concessional contributions you can make to a complying super fund each year that qualify for a tax deduction. The maximum permitted depends on whether you are under or over the age of 50.

condition of release   A condition you must satisfy before you can legally access your benefits in a superannuation fund. The most common condition of release is when you retire.

consumer price index (CPI)   The index that Australia uses to calculate its rate of inflation.

contracts for differences   A derivative that allows you to speculate in the price movement of underlying securities (such as shares) without actually owning them outright.

contributions tax   A 15 per cent rate of tax your super fund is liable to pay on before-tax concessional contributions you make to a complying super fund that qualifies for a tax deduction.

cost base   Under the capital gains tax provisions, the price you pay for CGT assets, such as shares, property and collectables. The cost base also includes your acquisition and disposal costs (for instance, stamp duty and agent's commission).

debentures   Medium- to long-term unsecured interest-bearing securities issued by companies. When you buy a debenture you are actually lending money to the issuing company. Debentures pay a fixed rate of interest during the term of the loan.

dividend franking credit   A tax credit (or tax offset) you receive from a dividend that is franked. The size of the credit depends on the company tax rate.

dividend yield   The rate of return on your investment in shares expressed as a percentage. The calculation is dividend per share ÷ market price of share × 100 = dividend yield.

exempt amount   Under the CGT concession for small business rule, a gain on the sale of business assets is exempt from tax. If you're aged less than 55, the capital gain must be paid into a complying super fund or retirement savings account (RSA). Individuals qualify for a $500 000 lifetime limit of exempt amounts.

financial planner   A licensed professional who can give you financial advice and prepare an investment plan for you.

financial year   Australia's financial year commences 1 July and ends 30 June each year.

fixed interest securities   Investments, such as term deposits, that pay you a fixed rate of interest over the term of the investment.

franked dividend   A dividend that entitles you to receive a dividend franking credit. The credit (or tax offset) is applied against the tax you are liable to pay. If no credit is received, the dividend is said to be unfranked. It is also possible for you to receive a partially franked dividend. This means only a certain percentage of the dividend will carry a credit.

goods and services tax (GST)   A 10 per cent tax on goods and services on your purchases and sales.

Government bonds   Interest bearing securities issued by federal and state governments that normally offer a fixed rate of interest during the term of the bond. When the bond matures, the bond holder gets back the amount initially invested, known as the face value. These bonds can be bought and sold on the ASX.

grossed-up dividend yield   The pre-tax rate of return on your investment in shares expressed as a percentage. The calculation is dividend per share + dividend franking credit ÷ market price of share × 100 = grossed-up dividend yield.

holding statement   A statement you receive from a company confirming the number of shares you own in that company.

income   Money you receive that is liable to income tax.

income tax   A federal tax that you must pay on income you derive.

Income Tax Assessment Act 1997 A collection of various tax acts that give the federal government the authority to levy a tax on taxable income.

income tax return A form you lodge with the ATO each year disclosing your taxable income.

industry funds A superannuation fund set up for specific industry. They are generally not-for-profit funds that are now open to the general public.

in-house assets A loan to, or an investment in, a related party (for instance, spouse) of the fund. In-house assets can also include a lease arrangement with a related party. The total market value of in-house assets cannot exceed 5 per cent of the market value of your super fund's total assets. This rule applies only to SMSFs.

in-specie contribution A non-cash contribution you make to your SMSF, such as transferring listed securities (for instance, shares listed on the ASX) or your business real property to your SMSF.

interpretative decision An ATO ruling relating to a specific tax issue.

interest A payment you receive for the use of your capital. Also a payment you make when you borrow money.

investment strategy A document that sets out how you intend to invest your benefits in an SMSF. It must be in writing and must consider, among other things, investment risks, the likely return on your investments, and whether you've got sufficient cash on hand to discharge liabilities when they fall due.

limited recourse borrowing   A borrowing arrangement an SMSF can use to purchase approved investment assets. Under this arrangement the investment asset is held in trust, and ownership will not transfer to your super fund until your fund pays the final instalment. In the event of default, the lender's right to recover any shortfall is limited to the specific asset in question.

listed securities   Asset classes such as shares, units, bonds, debentures, options, interests in managed investment schemes or other securities listed on the ASX that a member can transfer to an SMSF.

managed funds   Mutual or pooled investment funds managed by Australia's leading financial institutions (such as banks and insurance companies) that give investors the opportunity to invest in a wide range of domestic and foreign investment portfolios.

marginal tax rate   The rate of tax payable on the last taxable income dollar you earn. The rate can vary from 0 per cent to 45 per cent.

market value   The price a buyer is willing, but not anxious, to pay to a vendor, who in turn is willing, but not anxious, to sell if the asset was up for sale on the open market.

Medicare levy   A levy based on a percentage of your taxable income (currently 1.5 per cent).

member benefit statement   A statement you receive at least once a year from your super fund setting out the details of your account, such as member contributions, accumulated balance, investment earnings, tax payable and fees incurred, and the investment option you have selected to fund retirement strategies.

MySuper   A simplified low-cost, no-frills, default government-approved superannuation product that must meet certain conditions and will be offered by existing super funds. Employers must direct employee super contributions to this product if an employee does not choose a fund to accept employer superannuation guarantee contributions. MySuper is expected to be introduced from 2013.

no-TFN tax offset   Super fund members who do not supply a tax file number (TFN) are liable to pay 31.5 per cent additional tax on concessional contributions they make to their super fund. If you supply your TFN at a later date, you can claim a no-TFN tax offset in respect of the additional tax you paid in the past three years.

non–account based pension   Usually a lifetime pension, which means you're guaranteed a pension for the rest of your life. Your pension payments can only increase to counterbalance the impact of inflation.

non-commutable pension   A pension that can't be readily converted back into a lump sum cash payment. An example is a non–account based (or life) pension.

non-complying superannuation fund   A super fund that has not made an election to be regulated under the

Superannuation Industry (Supervision) Act 1993, or has failed to meet certain standards prescribed by the federal government. Non-complying super funds are liable to pay a 45 per cent rate of tax, instead of a 15 per cent tax rate on income.

non-concessional contribution A contribution you make to a complying super fund that does not qualify for a tax deduction. Also known as an after-tax contribution.

ordinary time earnings Under the superannuation guarantee provisions this means the total earnings you receive for the hours you have worked as an employee (such as salary and wages, overtime payments, allowances and bonuses). This is often called AWOTE—average weekly ordinary time earnings.

pay-as-you-go (PAYG) withholding tax An amount of tax that's withheld from regular income receipts (such as salary, wages and pensions) that are remitted to the ATO.

pension A regular retirement income stream you get from a complying super fund when you reach your preservation age and retire. Once you turn age 60 a super pension is ordinarily tax free and is excluded from your assessable income.

pension phase A phase that arises when a super fund stops accepting contributions from a member and the member's account converts into a pension account to meet pension payment obligations. Investment earnings and capital gains a super fund earns during the pension phase are exempt from tax.

preservation age   The age you must reach before you can access your superannuation fund benefits. Depending on when you were born this will be between 55 and 60 years of age.

preserved benefits   Superannuation fund benefits that you can access when you reach your preservation age and retire.

private ruling   Written advice you receive from the ATO about how it would interpret the law in respect of a tax issue you raise.

product disclosure statement (PDS)   A legal document that must be prepared when raising finance or offering a superannuation product. It will set out relevant information about the investment products, the benefits and risks, and the fees you will be charged.

property   Real estate, such as residential premises and commercial premises.

property trust   A managed fund that invests predominantly in major residential and commercial property developments located throughout Australia.

public sector funds   Superannuation funds set up specifically for public servants.

put option   A security that gives the holder the right, but not the obligation, to sell the underlying shares at an agreed price on or before the expiry date. A put option is worth buying in a falling market.

restricted non-preserved Superannuation fund benefits that you can access when you retire or satisfy a condition of release (for instance, you turn 60 and terminate your current employment).

retail funds Superannuation funds set up by Australia's leading financial institutions, such as banks and life insurance companies, that are open to the general public.

retirement savings account (RSA) A low-cost government-guaranteed savings account, managed by Australia's leading financial institutions that earn interest and charge minimal fees to manage your benefits. RSAs can accept superannuation contributions, such as employer superannuation guarantee contributions, and pay you a pension or lump sum on retirement. They cannot be released until you reach your preservation age and satisfy a condition of release.

reversionary beneficiary A nominated dependant who can continue to receive your super pension in the event of your death.

roll over Transferring your accumulated superannuation fund benefits between two complying superannuation funds. The sum transferred is called a rollover.

salary sacrifice Extra superannuation contributions to a super fund made by an employee from their pre-tax income. These are concessional contributions which will be taxed at 15 per cent instead of the employee's marginal tax rate if the money had been received in cash.

self-assessment The Australian tax systems works on a self-assessment basis. This means the onus is on the taxpayer to declare the correct amount of income earned each year, and to claim the correct amount of tax deductions and tax offsets.

self-employed A person who derives assessable income from operating their own business (such as a sole trader or partner in a partnership), rather than from being employed by someone and deriving a salary or wage.

self managed superannuation fund (SMSF) A superannuation fund that you set up and manage yourself. SMSFs are overseen by the ATO and must follow strict guidelines to retain their tax concessions.

severe financial hardship A condition of release that permits you to access some or all of your superannuation fund benefits if you get into financial difficulty and satisfy certain statutory conditions.

S&P/ASX 20 index A Standard and Poor's (a rating agency) index that comprises the top 20 companies listed on the ASX.

S&P/ASX 200 index A Standard and Poor's (a rating agency) index that comprises the top 200 companies and property trusts listed on the ASX.

shares Shares in a company make you a part-owner of the company, which entitles you to receive a dividend payment and a dividend franking credit.

share trust A managed fund that invests predominantly in shares listed on major stock exchanges, such as the ASX.

sole purpose test A test to check that the dominant reason for setting up a superannuation fund, including an SMSF, is to fund retirement benefits for members.

spouse contribution A superannuation contribution you can make to a complying super fund or retirement savings account on behalf of your spouse. These contributions qualify for a spouse contributions tax offset. Same-sex and de facto partners can also qualify for this offset.

stamp duty A state or territory government tax that applies to certain financial transactions you enter into, for example when you buy a commercial or residential property.

substantially self-employed A person who predominantly derives assessable income from operating their own business (for example, a sole trader or partner in a partnership) or from investments. Less than 10 per of the person's total assessable income comes from employment as an employee.

superannuation clearing house A free superannuation clearing house service administered by Medicare Australia. Employers who run a small business and have fewer than 20 employees can pay their super guarantee contributions electronically to one location. The clearing house forwards the contributions to the various super funds the employees have nominated to receive their contributions.

Superannuation Complaints Tribunal (SCT) An independent government tribunal authorised to resolve member disputes over certain decisions of trustees or the conduct of trustees of complying superannuation funds. Members of self-managed superannuation funds are ineligible to use this tribunal to resolve disputes. SMSF members need to take civil legal action to resolve disputes that may arise.

superannuation fund A fund set up to finance retirement strategies. Benefits in a super fund cannot be normally accessed until you reach your preservation age and retire from the workforce. A superannuation fund can pay you a pension or a lump sum when you meet a condition of release.

superannuation guarantee contribution A contribution to a complying superannuation fund that an employer is legally obliged to make on behalf of an employee. The amount is currently 9 per cent of what an employee earns.

***Superannuation Industry (Supervision) Act 1993* (SIS Act)** Federal legislation that gives the federal government the authority to regulate superannuation funds.

SuperSeeker An ATO search tool that allows superannuation fund members to look for lost or unclaimed superannuation benefits.

taxable component—taxed element Post–July 1983 accumulated benefits in a superannuation fund that are liable to tax. These payments are liable to tax when paid to the member, but are tax free once the member turns age 60.

taxable component—untaxed element Post–July 1983 accumulated benefits in a superannuation fund that haven't been taxed. These payments normally come from certain federal and state government superannuation schemes that don't pay tax, or from the proceeds of a life insurance policy. These payments are liable to tax when paid to the member.

taxable income The amount of income that is subject to income tax.

tax file number (TFN) A number you get from the ATO that you quote when you lodge a tax return or contact the Tax Office. Super funds need this number to help ensure your contributions are taxed at the lowest possible rate.

tax-free component Payments that are tax free and excluded from taxable income. They include non-concessional contributions and certain other super contributions, such as CGT-exempt components and pre-1983 accumulated amounts in super funds.

tax offset A tax credit that you can use to reduce the amount of tax payable (such as the 15 per cent tax offset deriving from a pension payable from a complying super fund if you're between 55 and 59 years of age).

Tax Office Ruling A public ruling issued by the ATO to explain and clarify how they interpret tax legislation in respect of a specific issue.

transition to retirement pension A superannuation pension that you can purchase when you reach your preservation age and continue working, whether full time or part time. The amount you can withdraw from your super fund each year must fall between 4 per cent and 10 per cent of the balance in your account.

trustee A person responsible for administering and managing a superannuation fund on behalf of the members. All members of a self-managed super fund must be trustees of the fund.

unfranked dividend A dividend that carries no dividend franking credits, indicating that the company was unable to pass on this franking credit to you (for instance, because it paid no tax on these earnings).

unrestricted non-preserved benefits Superannuation fund benefits that you can access immediately without satisfying a condition of release.

Appendix A

Key tax and superannuation rates

Australian tax rates

Table 1: individual tax rates for residents, 2011–12

Taxable income	Marginal tax rates
$0–$6000	0 per cent
$6001–$37000	15 per cent
$37001–$80000	30 per cent
$80001–$180000	37 per cent
Over $180000	45 per cent

Note: The Medicare levy of 1.5 per cent is added to these rates throughout this book.

Table 2: low-income threshold for the Medicare levy, 2009–11

	Low-income threshold	
Financial year	Individuals	Families
2009–10	$18488	$31196
2010–11	$18839	$31789

Note: The additional amount for each dependent child increased from $2865 to $2919 in 2010–11.

Table 3: low-income tax offset, 2010–12

Low-income residents are eligible for the low-income tax offset.

Year	2010–11	2011–12
Maximum tax offset	$1500	$1500
Taxable income threshold	$30000	$30000
Taxable income upper limit	$67500	$67500

Note: The low-income tax offset reduces by 4 cents for every dollar an individual earns above the taxable income threshold ($30000).

Australian residents who are eligible to receive a Commonwealth age pension or a Department of Veteran Affairs payment are eligible for the senior Australians tax offset.

Table 4: senior Australians tax offset, 2009–11

	Taxable income threshold	
Financial year	Single	Couple (each)
2009–10	$29 867	$25 680
2010–11	$30 685	$26 680

Note: The senior Australians tax offset reduces by 12.5 cents for every dollar above each threshold. If a member hasn't fully used the tax offset, the excess is transferable to the member's spouse.

Taxation of superannuation funds

- Complying superannuation funds: 15 per cent

- Non-complying superannuation funds: 45 per cent

- Supervisory levy: SMSFs must pay a $180 supervisory levy. The levy is added to the gross tax payable.

Superannuation contributions

Concessional contributions are pre-tax contributions you can make to a complying superannuation fund. They qualify for a tax deduction. They include employer contributions, salary sacrifice contributions and self-employed personal tax-deductible contributions.

Table 5: limits (caps) on concessional superannuation contributions for those less than 50 years of age, 2010–12

Financial year	Limit (cap)
2010–11	$25 000
2011–12	$25 000

Note: Concessional contributions that exceed the cap are liable to a 46.5 per cent rate of tax (including the Medicare levy).

Table 6: limits (caps) on concessional contributions for those over 50 years of age, 2010–12

Financial year	Limit (cap)
2010–11	$50 000
2011–12	$50 000

Note 1: Concessional contributions that exceed the cap are liable to a 46.5 per cent rate of tax (including the Medicare levy).

Note 2: From 1 July 2012 the cap amount for those aged 50 and above reverts to the under–50 years of age maximum cap amount. The federal Labor government has proposed retaining the limit of a $50 000 concessional contribution for those aged more than 50 years who have less than $500 000 in their superannuation fund.

Non-concessional contributions are after-tax personal contributions you can make to a complying superannuation fund. They do not qualify for a tax deduction.

Table 7: limits (caps) on non-concessional superannuation contributions, 2010–12

Financial year	Limit (cap)
2010–11	$150 000
2011–12	$150 000

Note 1: Non-concessional contributions that exceed the cap are liable to a 46.5 per cent rate of tax (including the Medicare levy). However if you are under 65 years of age you can contribute up to a maximum of $450 000 during the financial year. But you cannot make any further non-concessional contributions for the next two years.

Note 2: The non-concessional contribution cap is six times the under–50 years of age concessional contributions cap.

Table 8: maximum superannuation guarantee contribution base, 2009–11

Financial year	Amount per quarter	Amount per year
2009–10	$40 170	$160 680
2010–11	$42 220	$168 880

Note: Employers are not obliged to pay a super guarantee contribution on an employee's salary that exceeds the maximum superannuation guarantee contribution base.

Table 9: limits (caps) on capital gains tax (CGT) on non-concessional superannuation contributions, 2010–12

Financial year	Maximum CGT limit (cap)
2010–11	$1 155 000
2011–12	$1 205 000

Table 10: thresholds for superannuation co-contribution, 2010–12

Financial year	Low-income thresholds	High-income thresholds
2010–11	$31 920	$61 920
2011–12	$31 920	$61 920

Note 1: If your total assessable income is less than $31 920 and you make a $1000 non-concessional contribution to your super fund, the federal government will make a $1000 contribution in the following financial year to your complying super fund on your behalf.

Note 2: The co-contribution amount reduces at the rate of 3.333 cents for every dollar you earn above $31 920 and ceases if you earn more than $61 920.

Superannuation contributions tax offset

From 1 July 2013 if you earn less than $37 000, the federal government proposes to contribute up to $500 to your complying super fund on your behalf. This contribution is to eliminate the 15 per cent tax payable on concessional contributions to a complying superannuation fund, and it increases your balance in your superannuation fund.

Superannuation contributions splitting

Individual superannuation fund members can split concessional contributions made in the previous financial year with their (non-income or low-income earning) spouses or partners.

The maximum amount that can be split is 85 per cent of the concessional contributions cap.

The current superannuation guarantee (SG) rate is 9 per cent of an employee's ordinary time earnings (AWOTE). The federal Labor government proposes that the current superannuation guarantee rate will continue to apply until 2012–13. From 1 July 2013, it proposes increasing in the following stages.

Table 11: proposed increases for superannuation guarantee, 2013–20

Financial year	Superannuation guarantee rate
2013–14	9.25 per cent
2014–15	9.50 per cent
2015–16	10 per cent
2016–17	10.5 per cent
2017–18	11.00 per cent
2018–19	11.50 per cent
2019–20	12.00 per cent

Note: Currently the superannuation guarantee does not have to be paid for members aged more than 70 years. From 1 July 2013 the federal Labor government proposes to increase the age limit from 70 to 75 years of age.

Pensions

Table 12: minimum annual superannuation pension payments, from 2012

Age	30 June 2013 and after	30 June 2012
Under 65	4 per cent	3.0 per cent
65–74	5 per cent	3.75 per cent
75–79	6 per cent	4.5 per cent
80–84	7 per cent	5.25 per cent
85–89	9 per cent	6.75 per cent
90–94	11 per cent	8.25 per cent
95 and over	14 per cent	10.5 per cent

Note: For financial years ended 30 June 2009 to 2011 inclusive, the federal government reduced the minimum withdrawal requirements by 50 per cent for each age group. It was announced in the 2011–12 federal budget that a drawdown concession of 25 per cent will apply until 30 June 2012.

Table 13: preservation ages for access to superannuation benefits

Date of birth	Preservation age
Before 1 July 1960	55 years
1 July 1960 – 30 June 1961	56 years
1 July 1961 – 30 June 1962	57 years
1 July 1962 – 30 June 1963	58 years
1 July 1963 – 30 June 1964	59 years
From 1 July 1964	60 years

Superannuation pension tax offset

- *Ages 55 to 59 years.* If you're aged between 55 and 59 years and you receive a pension from a complying superannuation fund, you may qualify for a tax offset. The tax offset is equal to 15 per cent of the taxable component of the pension payment you receive.

- *Age over 60 years.* If you're aged over 60 years and you receive a superannuation pension from an untaxed source (for example, from certain federal and state government superannuation schemes), you can claim a 10 per cent tax offset on the untaxed component of the pension.

Superannuation spouse contribution tax offset

If your spouse's assessable income is $10 800 or less in a financial year, you may qualify for a $540 tax offset.

To qualify for the maximum tax offset, you must make a $3000 spouse contribution to a complying superannuation fund or retirement savings account (RSA) operated by an approved financial institution.

The tax offset reduces if your spouse earns more than $10 800 and ceases altogether if your spouse earns more than $13 800.

Lump sum superannuation payments

Table 14: limits (caps) on the untaxed part of superannuation lump sum payments, 2010–12

Financial year	Cap amount
2010–11	$160 000
2011–12	$165 000

Table 15: limits (caps) on superannuation lump sum payments from untaxed plans 2010–12

Financial year	Cap amount
2010–11	$1 155 000
2011–12	$1 205 000

Table 16: tax rates on lump sum superannuation death benefit payments

	Tax-free component	Taxable component
Dependant	Nil	Nil
Non-dependant	Nil	16.5 per cent

Note: If an untaxed component is paid to a dependant the whole amount is tax free. If an untaxed component is paid to a non-dependant, the whole amount is taxed at 31.5 per cent.

Table 17: tax rates on lump sum death benefit employment termination payments, 2010–12

Financial year	Lower cap amount (LCA)
2010–11	$160 000
2011–12	$165 000

Notes: If a taxed component is paid to a dependant, it is tax-free up to LCA. The amount above the LCA is taxed at a rate of 46.5 per cent.

If a taxed component is paid to a non-dependant, it is taxed at a rate of 31.5 per cent up to the LCA. The amount above the LCA is taxed at a rate of 46.5 per cent.

Appendix B

Key tax cases relating to superannuation

The following legal cases are often quoted and relied upon as authorities when dealing with common superannuation and taxation issues. You can find these cases on the Tax Office website at <www.ato.gov.au>.

Carrying on investment business
Share trading and super funds

Federal Commissioner of Taxation v Radnor Pty Ltd (1991) ATC 4689

Shields v Deputy Commissioner of Taxation (1999) ATC 4783

Contributions to super fund
No employment relationship

France v Federal Commissioner of Taxation (2010) ATC 10–158

Employees and independent contractors

Associated Translators and Linguists Pty Limited v Federal Commissioner of Taxation (2010) AATA 260

Brilliant v Federal Commissioner of Taxation (2010) AATA 267

Brinkley v Federal Commissioner of Taxation (2002) ATC 2053

Federal Commissioner of Taxation v De Luxe Red and Yellow Cabs Co-operative (Trading) Society Ltd & Ors (1998) ATC 4466

Hollis v Vabu Pty Ltd (trading as Crisis Couriers) (2001) ATC 4508

Stevens v Brodribb Sawmilling Co Pty Ltd (1986) 160 CLR 16

World Book (Australia) Pty Ltd v Federal Commissioner of Taxation (1992) ATC 4327

Employee knowledge of super fund

Bayton Cleaning Co Pty Ltd v Federal Commissioner of Taxation (1991) ATC 4076

Employer super contributions
In excess of salary derived

Ryan v Federal Commissioner of Taxation (2004)
ATC 2181

Financial assistance to members

*Deputy Commissioner of Taxation (Superannuation) v
Fitzgeralds & Anor* (2007) ATC 5105

Journal entries (superannuation and set-off payments)

Harmony and Montague Tin & Copper Mining (1873)
LR 8 LR Ch App 407

Loans and self-managed super funds

Eastern Nitrogen Ltd v Federal Commissioner of Taxation
(2001) ATC 4164

*Prime Wheat Association Ltd v Chief Commissioner of
Stamp Duties (NSW)* (1997) ATC 5015

ZDDD v Commissioner of Taxation (2011) AATA3
(10 January 2011)

Meaning (superannuation fund)

Mahoney v Federal Commissioner of Taxation (1967)
41 ALJR 232

Scott v Federal Commissioner of Taxation (No.2) (1966) 14 ATD 333

Walstern Pty Ltd v Federal Commissioner of Taxation (2003) ATC 5076

Provision for superannuation benefits

Raymor Contractors v Federal Commissioner of Taxation (1991) ATC 4259

Reimbursement of expenses incurred by trustees

RWG Management Ltd v Commissioner for Corporate Affairs (1985) VR 385

Residency test (self-managed superannuation funds)

CBNP Superannuation Fund v Federal Commissioner of Taxation (2009) ATC 10–105

Salary sacrifice arrangement and superannuation

Heinrich v Federal Commissioner of Taxation (2011) ATC 10–169

Self managed superannuation funds (breach of in-house rules)

JNVQ v Commissioner of Taxation (2009) AATA 522

Self managed superannuation funds
Death benefit payments

Donovan v Donovan (2009) QSC 26

Katz v Grossman (2005) NSWSC 934

Illegal access to super benefits

ASIC v Kossongo (MR 07–01)

Sole purpose test

Case 43/95 (1995) ATC 374 (Swiss Chalet case)

Federal Commissioner of Taxation v Roche (1991) ATC 5024

Special income
Dividends from private companies

Allen's Asphalt Staff Superannuation Fund v Federal Commissioner of Taxation (2010) ATC 20–225

Darrelen Pty Ltd v Federal Commissioner of Taxation (2010) ATC 20–180

Substantially self-employed (10 per cent rule)

Edmonds-Wilson v Federal Commissioner of Taxation (1998) ATC 2276

Falson v Federal Commissioner of Taxation (2007) ATC 2438

Norris v Federal Commissioner of Taxation (2002) ATC 2091

Northey v Federal Commissioner of Taxation (2002) ATC 2001

Prooyen v Federal Commissioner of Taxation (2010) ATC 10–132

Superannuation guarantee charge

Australian Communication Exchange Ltd v Deputy Federal Commissioner of Taxation (2003) ATC 4894

Brilliant v Federal Commissioner of Taxation (2010) AATA 267

Care Provider v Federal Commissioner of Taxation (2010) AATA 475

Commissioner of Taxation v Newton (2010) FCA 1440

Griffiths & Ors v Federal Commissioner of Taxation (2009) AAT Case AATA 482

Roy Morgan Research Pty Ltd v Federal Commissioner of Taxation (2009) ATC 10–106

Weston v Commissioner of Taxation (2008) 10–052

Superannuation Complaints Tribunal (leading cases)

Edington v Superannuation Complaints Tribunal (2010) FCA 504

Employers First v Tolhurst Capital Ltd (2005) FCA 616

Merkel v Superannuation Complaints Tribunal (2010) FCA 564

Tuftevski v Total Risks Management Ltd (2009) NSWSC 315

Vision Super Pty Ltd v Poulter (2006) FCA 849

Index

Also in this taxation and investment series

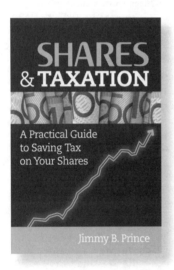

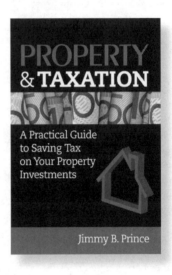

Available from all good bookstores